CONTRARY
TO
POPULAR
BELIEF

CONTRARY TO POPULAR BELIEF

Unwrapping the Mysteries of Faith

Stephen D. Hower

SAINT LOUIS

Library of Congress Cataloging-in-Publication Data

Hower, Stephen D., 1952-
    Contrary to popular belief/unwrapping the mysteries of faith /
Stephen D. Hower.
       p.   cm.
    ISBN 0-570-04989-X
    1. Christian life.   2. Theology, Doctrinal—Popular works.
3. Apologetics. I. Title.
BV4501.2.H616   1997
230—dc21   97-18657

1 2 3 4 5 6 7 8 9 10   06 05 04 03 02 01 00 99 98 97

Dedicated to those
who refuse to conform
for the sake of mere acceptance

Do not conform any longer to the pattern of this world, but be transformed by the renewing of your mind. Then you will be able to test and approve what God's will is—His good, pleasing and perfect will.
Romans 12:2

Contents

Prologue

The fourth-grade student returned smiling as he joined his parents after attending his first-ever Sunday school class. That was a good sign. It was a new experience for their son, and they were hoping it would go well. His folks, like many "thirty-something" Americans, were returning to their Christian roots after a fifteen-year leave of absence. Over breakfast at a nearby restaurant their son retold the lesson for the day.

"Dad you won't believe it," he began. "The Bible is cool. It's full of stories about war and violence, just like real life! Today our teacher told us how a general named Moses led a bunch of POWs out of an Egyptian prison to freedom. It was incredible. The whole Egyptian army followed them with tanks and stuff, but Moses was real smart. He led them through a huge oil field, which he blew up behind him. It took a long time for the tanks and troops to get around all the fires and smoke, which gave the POWs time to build a pontoon bridge and escape across a place called the Red Sea. But while they were still crossing, the Egyptians showed up and started to cross right behind them. It looked real bad for a moment, but Moses radioed ahead for help. Some Israeli screamers came zipping across the Sinai desert to the rescue. The enemy tanks and transports were smack-dab in the middle of the pontoon bridge when the jets blew them out of the water! The enemy was caught by total surprise and drowned in the middle of the Red Sea. It was cool!"

The father, who had more knowledge of the Bible than his son expected, listened politely until the boy's story was finished. "Son, I'm glad you enjoyed your class, but I don't think that's exactly how your teacher told the story, now is it?"

His son replied, "No. But if I told you the whopper he laid on us, you'd never believe it!"

The fourth-grader's observation hits the nail on the head. "If I told you the whoppers that Christians tell non-Christians, you'd never believe it!" Believers and nonbelievers are not connecting and it's confusing them both. What seems perfectly logical to Christians is by all objective standards ridiculous to nonbelievers. Christians don't understand why their friends reject what seems so clear, and non-Christians can't understand how otherwise reasonable and intelligent people have been sucked in by such simplistic notions of God, good, evil, and faith—their ultimate solution to all life's problems.

This book is written for Christians and those who want to know more about the strange things that Christians believe and do. Both Christians and their friends need to make some bold admissions. The Christian faith doesn't make sense. It is often illogical, incredibly simplistic, and requires a belief in the miraculous. No one can argue another person into the faith, and Christians should cease trying.

That doesn't mean that the faith cannot be defended. Reputable apologists have shown through verifiable historic prophecy and its fulfillment that God is as good as His Word. Credible archeologists have authenticated the historicity of the Bible over and over, often silencing skeptics who had previously argued that such battles, people, and cities could never be substantiated. The Christian faith is a historic faith and the centuries are littered with evidence of those who courageously lived out the events the Bible describes. The confusion of nonbelievers isn't always over the veracity of the Bible narratives. It often centers on the faith of those who made the history. Why did they live and die such sacrificial lives? The faith of the believer seems foolish to them, and the Bible agrees.

> For Christ did not send me to baptize, [wrote the apostle Paul,] but to preach the gospel—not with words of human wisdom, lest the cross of Christ be emptied of its power. For the message of the cross is foolishness to those who are perishing, but to us who are being saved it is the power of God. For it is written: "I will destroy the wisdom of the wise; the intelligence of the intelligent I will frustrate." Where is the wise man? Where is the scholar? Where is the philosopher of this age? Has not God made foolish the wisdom of the world? For since in the wisdom of God the world through its wisdom did not know Him, God was pleased through the foolishness of what was preached to save those who believe. (1 Corinthians 1:17–21)

During a Wednesday evening worship service I once asked all the young children to come forward for a short children's message. It was just a few weeks before Christmas and I was demonstrating to the children (and their parents who were craning their necks to see) how a family could conduct simple Advent devotions at home. After lighting the Advent wreath, I began to suggest ways Christian families could prepare their hearts for the coming celebration of Christmas. For the purpose of discussion I displayed an Advent calendar that my family had used when our boys were young.

An Advent calendar is often nothing more than a beautiful Christmas picture covered with numbered windows which are opened in sequence each day in December until Christmas. Ours sparkled with glitter, which enhanced a beautiful outdoor winter scene. Behind each perforated flap was a small picture and a biblical reference. The first picture showed Mary kneeling in prayer. The next was of the Angel Gabriel as he announced the coming birth to the young virgin. A third picture showed Mary on a journey with a reference to Luke 1:39–40. Before reading the passage, I asked the young audience where they thought Mary might be going to get ready for Jesus' birth. One young visitor answered in a clear and loud voice, "To the mall!"

What a great answer! Although contrary to the truth, her answer made perfect sense. That night was her first visit to a Christian church. Not more than four years old, she had been brought by neighbors who were members of the congregation. The members' own daughter, also very young, immediately "shhhhhssst" her friend, probably somewhat embarrassed by her answer. The congregation smiled and laughed spontaneously, which only confused our little visitor. She had answered well! It made perfectly good sense! To get ready for Christmas, mothers (and future mothers) go to the mall. I complimented her on her thoughtfulness and paraphrased the passage that told how Mary was actually going to see her relative Elizabeth who was also about to have a baby.

Christians should not expect non-Christian friends and family members to understand their faith. The things we believe and the things we do appear as foolishness to them, even *contrary to popular belief.* I have long observed how Christians, when confronted by such situations, seek out pastoral advice or conclude that something must be wrong with their ability to explain the faith in such a way that others would understand and accept it. Many Christians have read but have not appropriated Paul's explanation of conversion to the Christians at Corinth:

> We do, however, speak a message of wisdom among the mature, but not the wisdom of this age or of the rulers of this age, who are coming to nothing. No, we speak of God's secret wisdom, a wisdom that has been hidden and

that God destined for our glory before time began. None of the rulers of this age understood it, for if they had, they would not have crucified the Lord of glory. ... This is what we speak, not in words taught us by human wisdom but in words taught by the Spirit, expressing spiritual truths in spiritual words. The man without the Spirit does not accept the things that come from the Spirit of God, for they are foolishness to him, and he cannot understand them, because they are spiritually discerned. (1 Corinthians 2:6–8, 13–14)

The title of this book, *Contrary to Popular Belief,* describes why Christians and nonbelievers hold views which seem so sensible to the one and appear completely illogical to the other. The Christian faith is a never-ending paradox of attitudes and principles which, when considered objectively, seem rather foolish. "But," as Paul explains, "to those whom God has called, both Jews and Greeks, Christ [is] the power of God and the wisdom of God. For the foolishness of God is wiser than man's wisdom, and the weakness of God is stronger than man's strength" (1 Corinthians 1:24–25).

Not even Paul won them all. He knew that the battle for the hearts and minds of people was a spiritual one carried on in an unseen realm. He simply told the truth as his faith and God's Word permitted him to know it. He "preached Christ and Him crucified." He knew the results did not rest on his ability to speak or defend the faith but on the Holy Spirit who works through the Word.

Paul's inability didn't frustrate him, it brought him comfort. He was glad to know that the power to convert nonbelievers was not within his domain. "I came to you" he readily admitted, "in weakness and fear, and with much trembling. My message and my preaching were not with wise and persuasive words, but with a demonstration of the Spirit's power, so that your faith might not rest on men's wisdom, but on God's power" (1 Corinthians 2:3–4).

Understanding the principle of foolishness is essential to comprehending the wisdom of God, especially when that wisdom is *contrary to popular belief.*

CHAPTER ONE

In or Out

Christians living in a nonbelieving world

Jesus said, "My prayer is not that you take them out of the world but that you protect them from the evil one." John 17:15

How soon we forget. Take summers for instance. They are not what they used to be. I'm not referring to any overall change in temperature, rainfall, loss of the ozone, or some other environmental difference—summer's activities have changed. Summers are much quieter than they used to be. The summers of my youth were noisy. Before central air-conditioning people lived with their windows open, not closed. You could hear cars passing on the street, the neighbor's baby crying, lawnmowers roaring, and electric fans clattering as their blades clipped their protective guards. But loudest were the sounds of children playing, arguing, and running to tell mom about some unfairness or naughty word a friend said.

Neighborhood kids didn't come to the door and knock; they pressed their faces up to the screen door to ask if Johnny was home and could come out to play. In those days most moms took care of the homefront while dads went off to work, so the neighborhood was full of children. Wiffle-ball games lasted for days, called on account of darkness or because someone had to go visit Aunt Minnie and Uncle Carl. We wore a permanent baseball diamond in our backyard, and it doubled as a race track when too few kids showed up to play ball. Special rules applied. A ball hit in Bartroms' yard was an automatic out because they didn't care much for children or their games. A long ball into Kennedys' yard was a homerun because they didn't mind. Our field definitely favored right-handed pull-hitters.

We rode our bikes to the city park where college students, hired for the summer, taught us how to weave hotpads from fabric loops stretched across metal frames. We played softball and volleyball and made things from wood. On Saturdays we went to Tarzan matinees, swam in the quarry, or visited our grandparents on the farm.

Everywhere you went there were wooden screen doors, not the kind with pneumatic cylinders designed to quietly and slowly return a door to its closed position. No, screen doors were attached to long springs that groaned as they opened and twanged loudly as they recoiled, pulling the door after them. Doors didn't close, they banged. In frustration my father yelled, "Don't bang (at this point the door banged and his voice trailed off) ... the screen door." Realizing that children who left the house on a dead-run never actually heard the screen door bang, dad resorted to logic. When we reappeared to fetch some essential item or to gulp a drink of water, Dad urged, "Make up your mind. Either stay in or out!" We never complied and lived our summers in and out in nearly equal proportions.

The "ins and outs" of the Christian faith can be confusing to Christians and nonbelievers alike. Should Christians come *out* from the world, or should they acknowledge their proper place is *in* the world? Does the Lord, like a frustrated father, urge, "Make up your mind. Either stay in or out!"

The Bible is not silent on this point. In some areas Christians are not to be closely bound with nonbelievers. Paul told the Christians at Corinth,

Do not be yoked together with unbelievers. For what do righteousness and wickedness have in common? Or what fellowship can light have with darkness? What harmony is there between Christ and Belial? What does a believer have in common with an unbeliever? What agreement is there between the temple of God and idols? For we are the temple of the living God. As God has said: "I will live with them and walk among them, and I will be their God, and they will be My people."

"Therefore come out from them and be separate, says the Lord. Touch no unclean thing, and I will receive you. I will be a Father to you, and you will be My sons and daughters, says the Lord Almighty". (2 Corinthians 6:14–18)

In areas where decisions will be made about moral matters, it is best if Christians are not "bound together" with nonbelievers. Faithful Christians approach moral decisions with an assumption that there is right and there is wrong. Christians have God's Word to help them establish and maintain a moral center. Nonbelievers may or may not believe in moral absolutes and might be more inclined to decide matters on legality. For this reason Christian parents want their children to date and marry other Christians. Christian employees, while not expecting biblical truth to be the basis for decisions in the workplace, want to associate with firms that honor basic moral values. They want their companies to respect and view their Christian values as assets not detriments to corporate well-being.

But does maintaining the biblical standard of Christian integrity require isolation ("coming out") from the world? Not at all. In his letter to the Christians at Corinth, Paul made a distinction between the standards for which Christians are accountable and those held by the world in which we live, work, and rub elbows. Addressing the moral failure of a fellow Christian, he said, "I have written you in my letter not to associate with sexually immoral people—not at all meaning the people of this world who are immoral, or the greedy and swindlers, or idolaters. In that case you would have to leave this world. … What business is it of mine to judge those outside the church? Are you not to judge those inside? God will judge those outside. 'Expel the wicked man from among you' " (1 Corinthians 5:9–10, 12–13).

In effect, Paul was saying "It's okay to be in the world, just don't let the world get in you." What Paul was willing to tolerate among nonbelievers was quite different than the standards established for the Body of Christ. Christians hold one another accountable, but move without judgment among those who do not know the Lord or accept His ways. Lights are meant to be hung in dark places. If Christians are to be lights of faithfulness shining like a city upon a hill, they cannot retreat from the darkness. If forced to answer the challenge, "Either stay in or out. Make up your mind!" Christians would have to say, "I'll stay in *and* out. I choose to stay in the faith but live out in the world."

Paul urged the Christians at Corinth not to be bound together with unbelievers, but he also realized some were already in that situation. He urged those married to unbelievers to stay married and be godly influences on their spouses and witnesses to their children. (Cf. 1 Corinthians 7:10–16.) When Christians live authentic lives of faith in a non-Christian world, nonbelievers come to know Jesus Christ. Christians are in the world but not of the world. The Bible describes them as sojourners and exiles in a strange land (Hebrews 11:13–16). Christians have dual citizenship, guided first by their loyalties to Christ, but living also in a real world with its own standards and expectations.

In His longest recorded prayer, Jesus recognized this dual

citizenship of Christians who are loyal to the Lord yet integral members of society. He prayed, "My prayer is not that You take them out of the world but that You protect them from the evil one. They are not of the world, even as I am not of it. Sanctify them by the truth; Your word is truth" (John 17:15–17). Despite the good intentions of monastic orders, Jesus never intended His people to withdraw from evil. As the monastics found out, evil went with them in the guise of their own sinful nature. The solution is not isolation, but protection. Jesus prayed that His Father would protect His disciples as they lived and witnessed in a nonbelieving world. That protection comes through strengthened faith by means of God's Word.

By the time Danny Wuerffel ended his college career as quarterback for the University of Florida, he had established an outstanding reputation as a Christian athlete. He led his team to prominence and the right to play for the 1996–97 national championship against the only team that had beaten them during regular season play. Under Wuerffel's direction the Gators romped to a 53–point victory over the Florida State Seminoles, a convincing vindication of their earlier three-point loss. But what distinguishes Wuerffel from other all-stars goes much deeper than athletic prowess. Wuerffel is unashamedly Christian and openly credits his Savior for whatever success he has enjoyed.

A year earlier his team finished second in the nation after losing to Nebraska in the 1995 championship game. Even as a junior Wuerffel's skills were acknowledged by a third-place showing in the Heisman Trophy vote, college football's highest individual honor. He was also named the National Scholar-Athlete of the Year by no less than *Playboy* magazine. Wuerffel declined the award and the promotional opportunity it represented. Some were amazed. With millions in NFL contracts on the line, college athletes aren't in the habit of passing up notoriety. Wuerffel didn't hesitate. "It didn't take any thought at all. It would've been a lot of fun, and that's fine for some. I'm sure there's a good bit of the population out there that would think I'm silly for doing this. But there's also a good bit of the population that would understand that's not the type of person I want to portray myself as." Wuerffel knew how to be "in and out" at the same time—boldly living *in* his Christian faith while living *out* in the nonbelieving world.

When Wuerffel won the Heisman Trophy his senior year, his Christian principles remained intact. Before the glare of cameras and the crush of the national print media, Danny accepted the award by saying, "I just want to give all the glory and praise to God. He is the rock upon which I stand. Publicly, I'd like to ask Him to forgive me of my sins for they are many."[1]

Socrates once said, "The first key to greatness is to be in reality what we appear to be." What we are in public ought to closely resemble what we are in private. My favorite story on the question of integrity and honesty—especially regarding private reality and public perception—involves Lillian Carter, the well-known mother of former U.S. President Jimmy Carter. Miss Lillian, as she was often called, had a reputation for being outspoken, which gave Jody Powell, President Carter's press secretary, no end of trouble. As the story goes, without his approval she agreed to be interviewed by an especially aggressive female reporter looking for a story. That conversation went something like this:

> "Your son," the reporter began, "has been traveling the country telling people not to vote for him if he ever lies to them. Can you, knowing a son as only a mother can know her son—can you honestly say President Carter has never lied?"

"Well, perhaps a white lie," replied Miss Lillian.

"And what, please tell, is the difference between a white lie and a lie?" asked the reporter. "Define white lie for me."

"I'm not sure I can define it," replied Miss Lillian with a smile, "but I can give you an example. Do you remember when you came in the door a few minutes ago and I told you how good you looked and how glad I was to see you?"

The quality of a Christian's faith is judged by the degree of his or her integrity. When Peter behaved one way around Gentiles and another when Jews were present, his integrity and his Christian witness went out the window. Not only was Peter's witness compromised by his hypocrisy, his moral failure led to the downfall of others, even some of the most respected Christians of his day. The Gospel was at stake, and when Paul saw it, he held Peter accountable in front of everyone. "You are a Jew," Paul said, "yet you live like a Gentile and not like a Jew. How is it, then, that you force Gentiles to follow Jewish customs? ... So we, too, have put our faith in Christ Jesus that we may be justified by faith in Christ and not by observing the law, because by observing the law no one will be justified" (Galatians 2:14, 16).

The value of light is seen in contrast to the darkness around it. When lights grow dim their value is diminished. Christians are never asked by God to retreat to monastic communities to shield themselves from the world and all its trouble. It may not seem possible, but Christians are asked by Christ to live in the world without allowing the world to live in them. What is impossible for man is made possible by God.

CHAPTER TWO

War or Peace

How Christians deal with opposition

M

Do not repay anyone evil for evil. Be careful to do what is right in the eyes of everybody. Romans 12:17

ending Wall

Something there is that doesn't love a wall,
That sends the frozen-ground-swell under it,
And spills the upper bowlders in the sun;
And makes gaps even two can pass abreast....

I let my neighbor know beyond the hill;
And on a day we meet to walk the line
And set the wall between us once again.
We keep the wall between us as we go....

There where it is we do not need the wall:
He is all pine and I am apple-orchard.
My apple trees will never get across
And eat the cones under his pines, I tell him.
He only says, "Good fences make good neighbors."

Spring is the mischief in me, and I wonder
If I could put a notion in his head:
"Why do they make good neighbors? Isn't it
Where there are cows? But there are no cows.
Before I built a wall I'd ask to know

What I was walling in or walling out,
And to whom I was like to give offense.
Something there is that doesn't love a wall,
That wants it down!" ...

He will not go behind his father's saying,
And he likes having thought of it so well
He says it again, "Good fences make good neighbors."[2]

"A poem," Robert Frost once wrote, "begins in delight and ends in wisdom." His poem "Mending Wall" certainly qualifies. We resonate to his poetic opinion, "Before I built a wall I'd ask to know what I was walling in or walling out, and to whom I was like to give offense. Something there is that doesn't love a wall, that wants it down."

How best do we deal with the walls erected by others? Should we tear them down? Should we ignore them? Should we simply conclude, "Good walls make good neighbors," and leave them be? Should we make war or make peace?

During the darkest days of the Civil War, President Lincoln and Edwin Stanton, his secretary of war, spent countless hours in the telegraph office awaiting reports from the front lines. Stanton was a man of violent moods and was openly critical of Lincoln's leadership throughout his presidency. Stanton once joked that the famous explorer Paul Du Chaillu was foolish to wander about Africa trying to capture a gorilla when he could easily have found one in Springfield, Illinois, the president's hometown. Although Lincoln was aware of Stanton's criticism he kept him in office because he trusted his advice when it came to military strategy.

When General George McClellan, despite the advantage of superior forces, refused to advance his troops in the Florida campaign, Stanton was furious. He concluded his long-wind-ed verbal rampage by saying, "I'd like to write that man a letter and tell him what I really think of him." Lincoln supported the notion with one condition, before the letter was mailed the president wanted to review it. Stanton agreed.

Two days later the letter was finished and presented to Lincoln as he had requested. Stanton was surprised by the kind-hearted president's endorsement. "Well done," he said. "You told him in no uncertain terms exactly what you thought of his actions! Now what do you intend to do with your letter?"

"Why, dispatch it at once," Stanton replied.

"I wouldn't," replied the president. "I would throw it in the wastebasket. By writing the letter you got a load off your chest, and I'm sure you feel better. But if you send the letter you will only do yourself and our cause greater harm." The letter was thrown away as the president suggested and the secretary of war returned to more important duties.

Fighting fire with fire and giving as good as you get is not the way of wisdom. When Peter drew a sword to protect Jesus against Judas and the mob that came to arrest Him, Jesus told him, "Put your sword back in its place, ... for all who draw the sword will die by the sword" (Matthew 26:52). Even crusty Edwin Stanton presumably learned his lesson. At the bedside of the fallen leader, when the president died, he broke the silence with uncharacteristic grace. "There lies," Stanton said, "the greatest ruler of men the world has ever seen. Now he belongs to the ages."[3]

When assaulted, whether with words or blows to the body, there is a natural tendency to fight back. While the Bible does not advocate masochism, it does teach that the best way to handle injustice is kindness. "A gentle answer turns away wrath, but a harsh word stirs up anger" (Proverbs 15:1). Paul told the Christians at Rome,

> Do not repay anyone evil for evil. Be careful to do what is right in the eyes of everybody. If it is possible, as far as it depends on you, live at peace with everyone. Do not take revenge, my friends, but leave room for God's wrath, for it is written: "It is mine to avenge; I will repay," says the Lord. On the contrary: "If your enemy is hungry, feed him; if he is thirsty, give him something to drink. In doing this, you will heap burning coals on his head." Do not be overcome by evil, but overcome evil with good. (Romans 12:17–21)

No one should make the mistake of equating God's counsel to "leave room for the wrath of God" as doing nothing. Doing nothing and turning things over to God are not the same thing at all!

Two things happen when Christians refuse to engage the enemy and allow the Lord to "throw the blows." First, the sting goes out of the enemy's punches. The blows may come fast and furious, but they do little damage. Second, when evil people persist in their evil, God comes to the defense of the righteous.

The criticism of those who oppose the righteous will be seen for what it is: shallow, malicious, and wrong. When destructive gossip whirls around us like leaves in the autumn wind, God sends calm and then rakes the pile for burning. Solomon used a similar metaphor to describe the nullifying effect of God's care. "Like a fluttering sparrow or a darting swallow, an undeserved curse does not come to rest" (Proverbs 26:2). That is not to say good people won't listen to irresponsible gossip (and even pass it along). And yes, it hurts to watch friends get sucked into the rumors. But in the end, so long as your integrity remains intact, the false accusations will be seen for what they are, and those who perpetuate them will suffer the reproach. Meanwhile, the Bible reminds us to handle criticism "with gentleness and respect, keeping a clear conscience, so that those who speak maliciously against your good behavior in Christ may be ashamed of their slander. It is better, if it is God's will, to suffer for doing good than for doing evil" (1 Peter 3:15–17).

From the day he defeated Goliath until the day he died, David bore the brunt of great opposition. He knew how God protects the innocent and wrote, "The wicked draw the sword and bend the bow to bring down the poor and needy, to slay those whose ways are upright. But their swords will pierce their own hearts, and their bows will be broken" (Psalm 37:14–15). The Lord takes the offensive for the righteous and often destroys those who persist in evil. This is Scripture's second encouragement to turn false accusations and undeserved ill-will over to God.

Saul repeatedly tried to murder David and dispatched an army to track him down. Although God provided many opportunities for David to kill the evil king, he refused, preferring to leave his defense in the Lord's hands. He told Saul, "May the LORD judge between you and me. And may the LORD avenge the wrongs you have done to me, but my hand will not touch you" (1 Samuel 24:12). Both biblical principles are evident in the outcome. First, God protected David and, when Saul persisted in his evil, he was eventually destroyed. Knowing these principles makes me inclined to pray for my enemies rather than fear them.

The practical implications are significant. When the German composer and organist Max Reger received what he believed was an especially brutal and unfair critique in a published article, he had every right to be angry and blast his critic for his malicious words. Realizing the danger of such an approach, he took the criticism lightly and responded in humor. "Ich sitze in dem kleinsten Zimmer in meinem Hause. Ich habe Ihre Kritik vor mir. Im nachsten Augenblick wird sie hinter mir sein." (I am sitting in the smallest room of my house. I have your review before me. In another blink of the eye it will be behind me.")[4]

As Christians, our intention is to serve the Lord. Jesus was not dissuaded from His mission—not by Jewish criticism, not by a soldier's whip, not even by a Roman cross. He stuck to His course and accomplished His mission—the salvation of God's people. Paul said, "Consider Him who endured such opposition from sinful men, so that you will not grow weary and lose heart. In your struggle against sin, you have not yet resisted to the point of shedding your blood" (Hebrews 12:3–4).

The old proverb is true: "Ships surrounded by water are in no danger until they let the water in." Take it to the Lord. No one can hurt those who are protected by the almighty Creator of heaven and earth. When they criticize our ways, they draw attention to our witness. When they mock our faith, they cause others to think about Jesus. When they hurt us, they drive us to the Lord. And should they kill us, they set us free to enter the banquet halls of heaven!

It may not seem possible, but the greatest battles are often won without firing a shot.

CHAPTER THREE

Adding
or Subtracting

The danger of holding grudges

H*orgetting what is behind and straining toward what is ahead, I press on toward the goal to win the prize for which God has called me heaven- ward in Christ Jesus. Philippians 3:13–14*

ow much can one man take? When does the proverbial straw break the camel's back? Life is filled with heartache and hurt. No one escapes it. Some cope. Some break. What makes the difference? Maybe it's simple math. Some never learn to subtract.

Theodore John Kaczynski was very good at mathematics. So good in fact he skipped two grades and graduated from high school before he was old enough to drive. So good was Ted at learning that his family never had to worry about having enough funds to provide a quality education. He attended Harvard on a scholarship and was given the opportunity to do graduate work at the University of Michigan. His professors remember Kaczynski as a student obsessed with mathematics to the degree he thought of little else. They described his work as meticulous and original. His dissertation won an award and although only a student, Kaczynski had two articles published in academic journals, an accomplishment unheard of in his field. He wasn't just smart, he was brilliant. He wasn't just brilliant, he was a genius. Unfortunately, the great mathematical mind of Theodore John Kaczynski was not adept at subtraction. Addition without subtraction will kill you. The pains and heartaches of Kaczynski's life kept adding up until his brilliance turned to lunacy.

Socially awkward, Kaczynski found it especially difficult to relate to women. When his crass overtures were rejected by a female co-worker, Ted turned ugly. Lashing out with vulgar limericks which he posted in prominent places, the brilliant mathematician was fired from his blue-collar job. The man who fired him was his younger brother, David. It was about the same time that someone the newspapers nicknamed "The Unabomber" mailed his first lethal package to a professor at the University of Illinois, Chicago.

Sixteen bombings and 17 years later Ted Kaczynski was arrested and charged with a spree of violence that left three people dead and 23 maimed for life. When federal agents raided Kaczynski's remote wilderness hideout they found a wealth of evidence, including two bombs, handwritten notes listing past and future targets, and a typed copy of the now-infamous 35,000-word manifesto, which the Unabomber required *The Washington Post* and *The New York Times* to publish under threat of explosive consequences. The man who recognized Kaczynski's writing and brought an end to his reign of terror was again his brother David.

What turned a brilliant young man into an alleged anti-social, pathological criminal? Analysts now point to a series of traumas and rejections that turned a potentially productive life into a destructive force for evil.

- At six months of age Ted was isolated from contact with his parents for several weeks because of a life-threatening reaction to medication. Some say the baby's personality was noticeably altered by the incident. A once out-going baby became withdrawn.

- His mother stressed academics very early in Ted's life, almost completely ignoring the boy's social and emotional needs. She kept a journal on her brilliant son's achievements and urged his teachers to promote him to higher grades. Socially inept but academically brilliant, Ted now blames his mother for making him a misfit.
- But not everything that contributed to the strange behavior of Ted Kaczynski can be laid at the door of his childhood home. Ted's brilliance won a full-ride scholarship to Harvard. In an effort to "tone down" a campus party house, the university assigned Ted and a few other academics to the residence. That misguided strategy only drove Ted deeper into his self-imposed isolation. Richard Adams, a fellow student assigned to the same quarters, recalled, "I can picture him so well sitting there by himself, very taciturn. You'd be hard pressed to find anyone who thought of him as a friend. It's not our faulty memories. There was just nothing there."[5] Ted became known as the mathematics major with nothing positive to "add" to his campus living environment.
- Pursuit of a Ph.D. at the University of Michigan only widened the growing gap between Ted and the rest of society. He excelled at being different. Although he impressed his professors with theories and figures, he continued to struggle in the area of human relations. While his peers struggled to understand graduate-level mathematics, Ted published papers in professional journals. But every strength is its own weakness. A former professor recalled, "It was very difficult to carry on a conversation with him if it wasn't about mathematics."[6]

- Kaczynski's Ph.D., his commitment to excellence, his published work, and his track record for high honors landed the young doctor a professorship at the University of California at Berkeley. The drugged-out free-love culture of the mid-1960s was in full bloom at Berkeley. The counterculture was at extreme variance with the logic and order required of a mathematician. Without explanation or notice, Kaczynski resigned his position and retreated to the isolation of the Montana wilderness.
- His isolation intensified when his brother married and rejoined society after living an existence similar to Ted's in a remote part of Southwest Texas. That same year Ted's father committed suicide. Kaczynski was notified by letter, virtually his only form of contact with the outside world.

Life is full of pain and heartache, and Kaczynski certainly had his share. In commenting on the reasons behind Kaczynski's alleged criminal behavior, Jack Levin, a criminologist at Northeastern University, said if abuse and neglect were all that it took to produce such a warped perspective on life, we ought to have a whole world full of Unabombers. "It takes a lot more than a bad family life. Most likely, the Unabomber maimed and killed because of some lethal mixture of all these things, a critical massing of dark forces."[7]

The apostle Paul had a similar hard time in life. He wrote of it in his second letter to the Christians at Corinth:

> I have worked much harder [than the other apostles], been in prison more frequently, been flogged more severely, and been exposed to death again and again. Five times I received from the Jews the forty lashes minus one. Three times I was beaten with rods, once I was stoned, three times I was shipwrecked, I spent a night and a day in the open sea, I have been constantly on the

> move. I have been in danger from rivers, in danger from bandits, in danger from my own countrymen, in danger from Gentiles; in danger in the city, in danger in the country, in danger at sea; and in danger from false brothers. I have labored and toiled and have often gone without sleep; I have known hunger and thirst and have often gone without food; I have been cold and naked. Besides everything else, I face daily the pressure of my concern for all the churches. (2 Corinthians 11:23–28)

What was Paul's secret? Why didn't he go crazy? How did he handle the hardships, fight the good fight, and finish the race intact? Paul was in prison when he wrote to the Christians at Philippi. Despite his circumstance (not knowing whether he would live or die) Paul wrote an upbeat letter that is known today as his Epistle of Joy. The secret of Paul's ability to rise above circumstance is revealed in chapters three and four of that letter. In chapter three he wrote, "But one thing I do: Forgetting what is behind and straining toward what is ahead, I press on toward the goal to win the prize for which God has called me heavenward in Christ Jesus" (Philippians 3:13–14). In chapter four he explained, "I know what it is to be in need, and I know what it is to have plenty. I have learned the secret of being content in any and every situation, whether well fed or hungry, whether living in plenty or in want. I can do everything through Him who gives me strength" (Philippians 4:12–13).

Paul was able to subtract—able to forget the past and move on to the future. All the injustices and heartaches of life can easily overwhelm the most faithful Christian unless he or she can learn to let go of the pain. But how can you forgive and forget injustice as traumatic as Ted Kaczynski experienced? Paul said, "I can do everything through Him who gives me strength."

Don't attempt to forgive and forget emotional trauma based

on the worthiness of those who have hurt you. They may not want your forgiveness! They may be plotting even greater harm against you. They may very well be the rats you think they are. Christians forgive and forget because God has forgiven and forgotten their sins. Christians are able to forgive because they know that those who hurt others are often victims themselves. As He hung on the cross Jesus prayed for His executioners saying, "Father, forgive them, for they do not know what they are doing" (Luke 23:34). Had they truly understood who it was they were nailing to the cross, not even the threat of death would have been enough to make them comply. (Cf. John 1:11, Romans 1:21, and 1 Corinthians 2:8).

Have you ever studied the forgiveness of God? The Bible uses some very graphic picture language to describe the way God forgives our sins:

- Isaiah 43:25: "I, even I, am He who blots out your transgressions, for My own sake, and remembers your sins no more."
- Isaiah 38:17: "In Your love You kept me from the pit of destruction; You have put all my sins behind Your back."
- Micah 7:19: "You will again have compassion on us; You will tread our sins underfoot and hurl all our iniquities into the depths of the sea."
- Psalm 103:12: "As far as the east is from the west, so far has He removed our transgressions from us."
- Job 14:17: "My offenses will be sealed up in a bag; You will cover over my sin."

Did you notice the picture language? How does God handle sin? He blots it out, casts it behind His back, treads it underfoot, hurls it into the depths of the sea, sends it on a journey in the opposite direction, and seals it in a puncture-proof bag.

He can do all that because Jesus has paid the price. Paul said, "When you were dead in your sins and in the uncircumcision of your sinful nature, God made you alive with Christ. He forgave us all our sins, having canceled the written code, with its regulations, that was against us and that stood opposed to us; He took it away, nailing it to the cross" (Colossians 2:13–14).

We aren't in heaven yet. Paul even said he had not yet attained the goal even though he had been laid hold of by Christ. His secret for achieving the goal is critical. Remember? He said, "Forgetting what is behind and straining toward what is ahead, I press on toward the goal." Paul was able to forget. To put behind him the hardship and suffering while he pressed forward toward his goal. Paul was able to subtract hurt and heartache.

When I was learning the fine art of mathematics I had teachers who talked about subtraction by using the phrase, "take away." Four "take away" two equals two. Mrs. Bippus used a bowl with buttons to make her point. "Now Stephen," she said, "if you have four buttons in a bowl and you 'take away' two, how many buttons do you have left?" Even I could see there were only two buttons remaining.

Now just imagine that the buttons are hurts and heartaches. What would happen if you never "took away," never subtracted, but only allowed life to add more and more hurts and heartaches to your heart? How many buttons can a bowl hold before spilling over? How many hurts and heartaches can a heart endure before it breaks? And when it breaks, how many others will be hurt in the process?

Forgiveness in life, like subtraction in math, is critical to the equation. Those unable to subtract will reach their limits sooner or later. The Bible says, "Bear with each other and forgive whatever grievances you may have against one another. Forgive as the Lord forgave you" (Colossians 3:13). God knows that those unable to forgive others will end up destroying their own lives through bitterness and resentment. Notice that the motive is Jesus. Because He forgave us, we can forgive others. Forgiveness may seem inappropriate, even wrong. It is certainly contrary to popular practice. And it's true, many who hurt and harm others don't deserve to be forgiven. But unless we forgive and forget, the hurts and heartaches pile up, even multiply, until they destroy those who refuse to let go.

No one knew that Ted Kaczynski, the brilliant mathematician, had a problem with subtraction until it destroyed his life. No one knows the extent of your hurts and heartaches either ... at least not yet.

CHAPTER FOUR

Good or Evil

If God is so good, why is the world so bad?

How long will my enemy triumph over me? Look on me and answer, O LORD my God. Give light to my eyes, or I will sleep in death; my enemy will say, "I have overcome him," and my foes will rejoice when I fall. Psalm 13:2b–4

If God is good why is there so much evil in the world? The more you know the more cynical you can become. Take Solomon for instance.

Because of God's great love for David, and the difficult job facing the new young king, the Lord offered Solomon any request of his choosing. Solomon's answer is classic, "Now, O LORD my God, You have made Your servant king in place of my father David. But I am only a little child and do not know how to carry out my duties. Your servant is here among the people You have chosen, a great people, too numerous to count or number. So give Your servant a discerning heart to govern Your people and to distinguish between right and wrong. For who is able to govern this great people of Yours?" (1 Kings 3:7–9)

An inquisitive mind is a great gift, but a strength can also be a weakness. Solomon was intrigued by everything, especially what motivated people to behave in certain ways. He did not limit his investigation to observation and often indulged himself in every activity of the heart, both good and bad. The more he observed and the more he learned about people, the more cynical he became. In the book of Ecclesiastes we can learn from his experience.

> And I declared that the dead, who had already died, are happier than the living, who are still alive. But better than both is he who has not yet been, who has not seen the evil that is done under the sun. (Ecclesiastes 4:2–3)

> A good name is better than fine perfume, and the day of death better than the day of birth ... Consider what God has done: Who can straighten what He has made crooked? When times are good, be happy; but when times are bad, consider: God has made the one as well as the other. Therefore, a man cannot discover anything about his future. (Ecclesiastes 7:1, 13–14)

> Man's fate is like that of the animals; the same fate awaits them both: As one dies, so dies the other. All have the same breath; man has no advantage over the animal. (Ecclesiastes 3:19)

> There is something else meaningless that occurs on earth: righteous men who get what the wicked deserve, and wicked men who get what the righteous deserve. This too, I say, is meaningless. (Ecclesiastes 8:14)

> Then I saw all that God has done. No one can comprehend what goes on under the sun. Despite all his efforts to search it out, man cannot discover its meaning. Even if a wise man claims he knows, he cannot really comprehend it. (Ecclesiastes 8:17)

> All share a common destiny—the righteous and the wicked, the good and the bad, the clean and the unclean, those who offer sacrifices and those who do not. As it is with the good man, so with the sinner; as it is with those who take oaths, so with those who are afraid to take them. (Ecclesiastes 9:2)

According to Solomon's observation and experience we can conclude: Death is better than birth, but nonexistence is better yet. Man's future is and always will be a mystery. We must take the good with the bad and will rarely understand why God allows either one to occur. Man has no advantage over animals. We may be smarter than animals but death awaits us just the same. Good things happen to bad people and bad things happen to good people and no one really knows why. The same fate seems to happen to both righteous and unrighteous people. The righteous apparently have no advantage.

Solomon's sentiments are not as isolated as Christians might like to think. Before we judge his skepticism we must admit our own moments of doubt and confusion. His candor captures the common disillusion that Christians and nonbelievers sometimes feel about unexplainable tragedies that strike entire populations without consideration of who is good or who is evil.

Take the Johnstown flood for instance. Who can explain why more than 3,000 unsuspecting people died in a matter of seconds? More than 1,000 of their bodies were never found.

It happened without warning on May 31, 1889, as school was ending for the day. The sleepy Pennsylvania town in the beautiful Allegheny Mountains never knew what hit it. After heavy spring rains, a 72-foot-high, 300-yard-wide earthen dam gave way. The largest man-made lake in North America, containing 20 million tons of water, broke free and began its 14-mile journey toward the unsuspecting town. The water swept along everything in its path, entire hillsides and everything on them: animals, people, trees, buildings, schools, factories, 80-ton steam locomotives with their railroad cars. The churning carnage pushed ahead of the water and slowed its progress but did nothing to diminish its force. When the wall of water finally reached Johnstown there was no escape.

News reports told incredible stories of survival and death. The Gautier Wire Works was swept away, spewing 200,000 pounds of barbed wire into raging currents to entangle and kill all in its path. Horace Rose, crippled by the crush of his house, managed to ride out the flood with his entire family on the roof of their house. By contrast, Mrs. John Fenn watched her husband and each of her seven children drown as their house broke apart. Holding on to a barrel she was pulled to safety but asked, "My God, what have I to live for?" More than 18 hours after the destruction of Johnstown, workers began pulling corpses from the Allegheny River in Pittsburgh, 75 miles below the dam. They pulled ashore the remnants of a house containing an unharmed five-month-old infant whose parents were never found.[8] How can anyone explain such indiscriminate devastation? Why were some spared and others lost?

So common and confusing is this issue that Jesus was asked directly about such situations during His ministry. When told about some Galileans who were indiscriminately killed by some of Pilate's soldiers as they made their sacrifices at the temple, Jesus said, "Do you think that these Galileans were worse sinners than all the other Galileans because they suffered this way? I tell you, no! But unless you repent, you too will all perish. Or those eighteen who died when the tower in Siloam fell on them—do you think they were more guilty than all the others living in Jerusalem? I tell you, no! But unless you repent, you too will all perish" (Luke 13:2–5).

Solomon is right to say that good and evil come to all people and it has little to do with a person's state of faith. It should, Jesus said, serve as a reminder that life is fleeting and tomorrow is never guaranteed. Instead of asking why such tragedies occur, Christians might spend more profitable time contemplating the grace of God and asking why anyone escapes God's righteous wrath and judgment of sinners. As the Bible says, "The soul who sins is the one who will die ..." and "There is no one righteous, not even one" (Ezekiel 18:20, Romans 3:10). By virtue of sin, death of the most tragic kind is what all sinners deserve. But God, by means of His grace, spares all who take shelter through faith in His Son, Jesus.

We need to give credit where credit is due. When God finished creating the world He stepped back and admired its perfection. "God saw all that He had made, and it was very good" (Genesis 1:31). God is not in the evil-creating business. The earth that God made and all it contained was good—only good. Through the temptation of Adam and Eve, Satan brought the tragedy of sin with all its evil offspring into existence. The tragedy of natural disasters reminds us that people weren't the only ones to endure the consequences of sin. Paul says, "The whole creation has been groaning as in the pains of childbirth right up to the present time" (Romans 8:22). The thorns and thistles growing in Adam's fields were symptomatic of greater changes.

It was Satan, not the Lord, who enticed earth's first inhabitants to join him in misery. As James reminds us, "God cannot be tempted by evil, nor does He tempt anyone; but each one is tempted when, by his own evil desire, he is dragged away and enticed. Then, after desire has conceived, it gives birth to sin; and sin, when it is full-grown, gives birth to death" (James 1:13–15). Sin has had ample time and sufficient nurture to become full-grown.

If God is not the cause of evil, then why doesn't He end it? Perhaps God isn't good, or maybe He isn't almighty. Jesus explained the coexistence of evil and good in a simple parable about farming. The actual story is recorded in Matthew chapter thirteen.

A good farmer sowed good seed in a good field. But while his servants were sleeping, an enemy came and sowed weeds in the middle of his crop. The weeds disguised themselves like the crop until later when their true character became known. The farmer's servants came to their master and asked for his advice on removing the weeds and sparing the crop. Should they pull the young weeds up or wait until the harvest?

The farmer knew that allowing the weeds to grow in the middle of the crop would affect his harvest by indirectly affecting his plants. The presence of weeds produces stunted growth and a less bountiful harvest. The weeds steal precious nutrients from the soil and compete with the good crop for sunshine and moisture. On the other hand, if the servants walked through the field and uprooted the young weeds, they would surely also destroy some of the farmer's crop. By now the weeds and the crop had roots that entwined. To uproot the one was to risk destroying the other. What would the wise farmer do?

Out of love for every plant in his field, the conscientious farmer decided to let the weeds and his crop grow side by side until the harvest. The farmer could not endure the thought of destroying even one of his precious stalks. He would rather have less productivity with more plants than more productivity with fewer plants.

Of course the story Jesus told is about people, not plants. The heavenly Father is the compassionate farmer who realized the consequence of allowing good people to live side by side with evil people. Good people will endure evil and evil people will benefit from their association with the good. It should be noted that God's definition of "good people" is technical. In His book it means perfect people, namely people made perfect through faith in Jesus. While believers and nonbelievers can both do "good things," only believers are considered good in God's sight. The Bible says, "Without faith it is impossible to please God, because anyone who comes to Him must believe that He exists and that He rewards those who earnestly seek Him" (Hebrews 11:6). The good news is that God is not prejudiced. He does not discriminate. He desires "all men to be saved and to come to a knowledge of the truth" (1 Timothy 2:4).

As Jesus' parable reveals, God knows that if He suddenly destroyed those outside saving faith, many Christians might also be lost. Our lives are entwined by love to many who are not a part of God's family. A blow against people we love would shake many Christians to their roots and even destroy the faith of some. God loves every individual too much to allow even one to be lost. Until "the crop" is separated on the final day, good and evil will grow side by side in a world of injustice. But on that day the faithful will be gathered into heaven, and the rest will be consigned to hell.

Good and Evil

Good and evil grow side by side,
Such is the truth of life.
For the good with the evil must endure
The sorrow, the hate, and strife.

Life is not fair as pain we bear,
Along the narrow way.
But good can endure, for faith is sure,
That leads to that Glorious Day.

Until that glorious day, good and evil must coexist, each experiencing the consequence of the other's actions. God's approach seems contrary to popular belief that a good God should immediately destroy any and all evil. Knowing the future helps. With the apostle, Christians can say, "I consider that our present sufferings are not worth comparing with the glory that will be revealed in us" (Romans 8:18).

Even Solomon looked forward to the day when good and evil would be separated once and for all. After a lifetime of observation and personal experience, he summarized life with these words: "Now all has been heard; here is the conclusion of the matter: Fear God, and keep His commandments, for this is the whole duty of man. For God will bring every deed into judgment, including every hidden thing, whether it is good or evil" (Ecclesiastes 12:13–14).

CHAPTER FIVE

Miracles or Magic

Are miracles for real?

As you do not know the path of the wind, or how the body is formed in a mother's womb, so you cannot understand the work of God, the Maker of all things. Ecclesiastes 11:5

'm one of those Baby Boomers you read so much about. Born after our fathers came back from WW II, we grew up during the golden age of television. My family lived twenty-five miles from the nearest television broadcast tower, and our house was tucked behind a hill. It was not easy to get a good picture on Stultz road. I can still remember my father sitting astride the peak of our two-story house, twisting the antenna pipe, and yelling down to Mom, "How about that? Is that any better?"

"No. No better," Mom shouted back.

"How about that? That *has* to be better," he replied.

"I don't know." Mom's voice faltered, then she turned to one of my older sisters and asked if she thought it was any better.

"Maybe it's because the wire is touching the house," Dad said.

Then he climbed down and began screwing long insulated standoff screws into the slats of the clapboard siding. If a ball game was playing on the "hard-to-reach" channel he might climb up on the roof just to turn the antenna for that one game. Some people had mechanical rotators that turned the antenna without risking life and limb. For some reason Dad preferred to climb, so we grew up with one section of a wooden ladder leaning against the kitchen roof on the back of the house. From there it was just a short hop to the peak of the second story.

Those were the days when televisions had something called "converters" on top of the actual television sets. The converters I remember were the size of tabletop radios and were made of plastic. Like some kind of medieval remote control, they served the purpose of changing channels before tuners were built into the actual cabinets. Our converters always had the tops broken off. Dad thought it helped the picture to give the converter a good slam every now and then.

The television itself was a huge thing filled with tubes that glowed the prettiest orange when everything was working. The picture tube was as deep as it was wide—maybe deeper. The horizontal and vertical hold knobs were rubbed shiny from constant adjustment. The picture always seemed to stop rolling when you touched the knob and start rolling again by the time you got back to your chair. Sometimes we arranged the chairs in patterns that seemed to help the reception. Sometimes we made our youngest brother sit by the TV to hold the knobs just so.

Everyone in our neighborhood had a strip of aluminum foil wrapped around the antenna wire which they slid up and down to help clear away the "snow." It was always snowing on our TV. It didn't matter if it was Lloyd Bridges in *Sea Hunt* or Gabby Hays standing by a chuck wagon. I grew up believing it must snow a lot in California where all my favorite shows were made. I must have been ten before I realized it was a transmission problem, not a weather condition.

Those were the days of test patterns and "late-night" sign-offs. The test pattern was a bulls-eye-looking symbol that supposedly helped everyone tune their televisions to the sharpest possible focus. The "sign-off" was that time when your local channel went off the air announcing, "This concludes our broadcast day." "The Star Spangled Banner" was played or sung as pictures of flapping flags and military maneuvers filled the screen. In the 1950s television stations worked under the assumption that everyone had fallen asleep before the sign-off time. To wake us up and send us to bed, they blared the national anthem at four or five times the decibel level of the previous program. If you were a fourteen-year-old trying to stay up past your bedtime, your mom would hear the sign-off and catch you. (I think the PTA and our moms actually paid the local station to play the sign-off at an extra loud level.)

Although we enjoyed many weekly programs at home, there were two shows every year that required "off-site" viewing. Uncle Brice and Aunt Maxine had no children of their own so they went out of their way to entertain and help their nieces and nephews. Each year when *The Ten Commandments* and *The Wizard of Oz* were broadcast, they invited us to watch television at their home. Brice and Maxine were the first people we knew who had color TV. It amazed us. Cecil B. DeMille's 1955 version of *The Ten Commandments* was spectacular. We actually saw Moses part the waters of the Red Sea while a pillar of fire kept Pharaoh's army at bay. When the walls of water collapsed on the Egyptian army, an audible gasp went up across the room. Swirling fireballs flamed from heaven, carving tablets out of stone on Mount Sinai. Moses, I was convinced, must look like Charleton Heston with a beard.

So excellent was DeMille's production, it was impossible for a child to separate fact from fantasy. Were they really miracles or magic? If Cecil B. DeMille could fool a generation with special effects, couldn't God and the prophets who spoke for Him?

The Wizard of Oz only deepened our quandary. In the end, Toto unmasked the Wizard, proving him a mere mortal. Dorothy awoke from her sleep confused. What was real and what was not? What was miracle and what was magic? The Baby Boomers are not as willing to believe as they once were.

The Bible acknowledges the reality of magic and deception. When Aaron threw his staff down before Pharaoh it was miraculously transformed into a serpent. Pharaoh was not impressed. He called for his own magicians who repeated the phenomenon by means of their "secret arts." Though Aaron's serpent swallowed the others, Pharaoh remained unconvinced. Egypt's magicians matched Moses wonder for wonder and sign for sign. They changed water into blood and brought frogs out of their hiding places to invade the land. No wonder nonbelievers question the reality of miracles! A good magician can baffle the most doubtful skeptic with unexplainable signs and wonders. But there is one big difference between miracles and magic. Magicians always reach their limit. God has none.

After the plague of frogs, the magicians of Egypt could no longer keep up with Moses. When he transformed the dust of the earth into pestering gnats, the magicians conceded. They even told Pharaoh, "We know magic. This is not magic. This is the finger of God!" (Cf. Exodus 8:18–19.)

Even the Bible acknowledges there is power in the world besides the power of God. Angels have power. When Sennacherib came out of Assyria to destroy Israel and threaten

Judah, God sent a destroying angel. During the night one angel destroyed 185,000 Assyrians as they slept. For good reason Paul warns Christians, "Be strong in the Lord and in His mighty power. Put on the full armor of God so that you can take your stand against the devil's schemes. For our struggle is not against flesh and blood, but against the rulers, against the authorities, against the powers of this dark world and against the spiritual forces of evil in the heavenly realms" (Ephesians 6:10–12). Angels have great power. The angel of God destroyed Sennacherib's army. Paul warns Christians to be careful of evil angels.

But if God is God, and angels are only created beings inferior to God, why are evil angels permitted to perform wonders and signs that might confuse and misguide Christians and nonbelievers? Moses predicted it would happen. In his farewell sermon just before his death, Moses cautioned the people about following leaders who "proved themselves" by miracles and magic.

> If a prophet, or one who foretells by dreams, appears among you and announces to you a miraculous sign or wonder, and if the sign or wonder of which he has spoken takes place, and he says, "Let us follow other gods" (gods you have not known) "and let us worship them," you must not listen to the words of that prophet or dreamer. The LORD your God is testing you to find out whether you love Him with all your heart and with all your soul. It is the LORD your God you must follow, and Him you must revere. Keep His commands and obey Him; serve Him and hold fast to Him. That prophet or dreamer must be put to death, because he preached rebellion against the LORD your God, who brought you out of Egypt and redeemed you from the land of slavery; he has tried to turn you from the way the LORD your God commanded you to follow. You must purge the evil from among you. (Deuteronomy 13:1–5)

Christians and those who seek truth should not be overly impressed by miracles and magic. As we've seen, angels—good and bad—have great power. Magicians, for good or evil, can fool and entertain us by their slight of hand and "secret arts."

Throughout the Bible's long history, miracles grabbed the attention of believers and nonbelievers alike. When Pharaoh's chariots were drowned in the Red Sea, the Israelites sang, "Who among the gods is like You, O LORD? Who is like You—majestic in holiness, awesome in glory, working wonders?" (Exodus 15:11)

During the days of Daniel, when the Babylonian king Nebuchadnezzar realized that God had spared the lives of Shadrach, Meshach, and Abednego from his fiery furnace, he said, "Praise be to the God of Shadrach, Meshach and Abednego, who has sent His angel and rescued His servants! They trusted in Him and defied the king's command and were willing to give up their lives rather than serve or worship any god except their own God. Therefore I decree that the people of any nation or language who say anything against the God of Shadrach, Meshach and Abednego be cut into pieces and their houses be turned into piles of rubble, for no other god can save in this way" (Daniel 3:28–29).

The New Testament miracles of Jesus were also used by God to bring attention to the truth He proclaimed. Shortly after Jesus began to appear in public, a high-ranking Jewish official named Nicodemus came to Him at night. Nicodemus came at night because he wanted to avoid the criticism of his peers. He came at all because, as he told Jesus, "Rabbi, we know you are a teacher who has come from God. For no one could perform the miraculous signs You are doing if God were not with Him" (John 3:2). The miracles of Jesus captivated his attention but it was the message of Jesus that saved Nicodemus' life. Jesus told Nicodemus, "I tell you the truth, no one can see the kingdom of God unless he is born again" (John 3:3).

The centurion who supervised the crucifixion of Jesus was amazed by the miracles that accompanied His death. Earthquakes shook the ground, holy people were raised from the dead, and the sky became black as night. The miracles captured his attention but he was saved by faith in the One who caused the miracles. Moved by the spectacle, the words of Christ, and the debate that swirled about Christ's true identity, he could only conclude, "Surely He was the Son of God!" (Matthew 27:54)

Are there such things as miracles? Absolutely. The Bible is filled with stories of miracles in both the Old and New Testaments—ax heads floating in water, blind people receiving their sight, crippled people walking, and the dead rising to life. Nonbelievers might argue that the Bible is wrong and the stories aren't true, but they could never argue that the Bible doesn't claim that real miracles occurred for which there are no possible earthly explanations. From the parting of the Red Sea to the resurrection of Jesus on Easter morning, the Bible boldly claims that God can and does perform miracles on earth. The Christian faith is founded on the greatest miracle of all, "The Word [God's Son] became flesh and made His dwelling among us. We have seen His glory, the glory of the One and Only, who came from the Father, full of grace and truth" (John 1:14).

Wherever God goes, miracles follow. When the disciples heard the discussion Jesus had with the young rich man and saw the standard required for salvation they asked with astonishment, "If this is what is required, then who can be saved?!" (Matthew 19:25, paraphrase) Jesus' response is as valid today as it was then: "With man this is impossible, but with God all things are possible" (Matthew 19:26). Every time someone accepts Jesus as his or her personal Lord and Savior, God has been at work accomplishing a miracle.

As Moses cautioned in Deuteronomy 13 (see above) signs and wonders should not be the sole basis for determining whom you trust and whom you don't. Even Satan can perform miracles, and he delights in deceiving gullible Christians. (Cf. 2 Corinthians 11:14–15.) "What is true?" not "What is miraculous?" is the most important question for the Christian to ask. Jesus warned, "Many will say to Me on that day, 'Lord, Lord, did we not prophesy in Your name, and in Your name drive out demons and perform many miracles?' Then I will tell them plainly, 'I never knew you. Away from Me, you evildoers!' " (Matthew 7:22–23)

Paul told Christians of his day, "When I was a child, I talked like a child, I thought like a child, I reasoned like a child. When I became a man, I put childish ways behind me" (1 Corinthians 13:11). When I was a child, the miracles and wonders of TV impressed me. I couldn't tell what was real from what was pretend. I'm not a child anymore.

CHAPTER SIX

Holidays
or Holy Days

Should Christians keep the holidays?

J *"Everything is permissible"—but not everything is beneficial. "Everything is permissible"—but not everything is constructive. 1 Corinthians 10:23*

ay Leno began one October 31st monolog by telling the audience how frustrated he was with the way Americans celebrate Halloween. "It has become so secular," he lamented tongue-in-cheek. "I'll bet none of you even worshiped Satan today! The religious significance is lost! All Halloween means anymore is candy, costumes, and parties! It just isn't like it used to be."

Jay's comments were humorous because they parodied what many Christians say about the celebration of religious holidays. The significance of Christ's birth is lost on Santa Claus, the importance of Jesus' resurrection competes with a bunny who hides painted eggs, and the Reformation has been displaced by a night of trick-or-treat.

I'll never forget my first year in the ministry. Everything was new for me. I conducted my first baptism, performed my first wedding, officiated at my first funeral, and experienced my first holidays from the other side of the pulpit. My first assignment was a small congregation in the "middle of the mitten." (That's Michigan talk for the center of the state.) I was installed during July and was still getting acquainted when the schedule began moving rapidly towards the holidays.

For Lutheran Christians, the holidays begin early. While the rest of Christendom begins the season at Thanksgiving, we kick things off with the celebration of Reformation Day on October 31. All Hallows' Eve, as it was called in Martin Luther's day, was like Christmas Eve has become for Americans. Everyone went to church. Believing that the saints in heaven could make intercession for the living, they held in high regard a night designated to honor all saints. Those who worshiped on All Hallows' Eve had every reason to believe their prayers would receive special attention. Because the night promised a big crowd, Luther chose October 31st to post on the castle doors at Wittenburg his ninety-five reasons for opposing indulgences and other church abuses.

During my four years as a student on the campus of a prestigious Lutheran seminary, Reformation Day was celebrated in a big way. Every October 31st brought a packed house as faithful Lutheran Christians gathered to hear a rousing sermon on justification by grace through faith alone. I couldn't wait to conduct my own Reformation service in my new congregation. I spent weeks planning the service and the message.

Things did not go as I had planned. I should have guessed we were in trouble when the youngest elder of the congregation brought his preschooler by the parsonage for trick-or-treat just as I was preparing to leave for church. I was wearing a clerical collar and a black suit when I answered the door.

"Trick or treat," he said with a big smile and began showing off the cute costume his wife had made for their child.

"And a blessed Reformation Day to you!" I responded. My wife, Carol, eased the moment with niceties about how cute the child looked and asked the young mother, "Did you sew that yourself?"

My memory is not what it used to be, but I recall the young man took a good look at my "uniform" and asked if I was going trick-or-treating dressed like a Catholic priest. I don't remember what I said, but I can imagine what I thought.

The Reformation service was supposed to begin at 7:00 p.m. I remember wondering if the people had mistakenly thought it was scheduled for 7:30 p.m. Apparently not. When 7:30 came, the organist, her husband, and Carol were still my only audience. (I've kept every sermon I've ever preached. Some day I'm going to pull that one out and preach it again. It still has a lot of tread on the tires.) I remember the laughter and sound advice of my father-in-law when we called to wish him "Blessed Reformation" later that evening: "Stephen, you'll be a year older but a whole lot wiser next time." He has said that same thing often over the years.

Today, even fewer Lutheran churches celebrate Reformation Day with an October 31st evening service—probably only those on Lutheran seminary campuses or those pastored by first-year graduates. Older and wiser pastors still celebrate the occasion but prefer to hold the service the Sunday before the historic date. They reason that the best celebrations are services that actually have participants in the pews.

So what's the solution? Has the world taken over? Should we run out into the wilderness and cry like Elijah, "I have had enough, LORD. ... Take my life; I am no better than my ancestors ... I have been very zealous for the LORD God Almighty. The Israelites have rejected Your covenant, broken down Your altars, and put Your prophets to death with the sword. I am the only one left!" (1 Kings 19:4, 10)

Asking God to put us out of our misery is not the answer. The encroachment of the world is no threat to the faith of the true believer. The world has nothing to offer equivalent to God's gifts at Christmas, Easter, and the Reformation. Faithful Christians (and first-year pastors) shouldn't feel compelled to choose between the two. By definition, they are not the same. One celebration is spiritual, and the other is not. As Christians we should welcome the world's desire to join in the observance and use it as a teaching opportunity, inviting the unchurched to discover the real meaning of the season. Christians, under certain conditions, can likewise join in celebrating our nation's traditions without guilt or sin.

The apostle Paul lived at a time when false gods and false teachers were more plentiful than Christians. You can imagine the questions he had to answer on the subject of compromise. "As a Christian can I participate in anything that might associate me with false gods even though I don't believe in them? How do we handle it when our husbands want to celebrate the local customs but we aren't sure we should? What do we tell our children?"

During Paul's day, some Christians were purchasing and eating meat that had been offered to idols. Other Christians objected, arguing that Christians who purchased meat offered to idols were participating in pagan worship and giving a false witness. Those buying the sacrifices thought such a view was ridiculous. They didn't believe in false gods and the other Christians knew it. They were only buying the meat because it was a good deal. To them, meat was meat. Paul was asked to decide who was right and who was wrong.

Paul gave three answers to this question.

First and foremost he affirmed, Christians are free. "Food is just food," Paul said. "It does not bring us near to God; we are no worse if we do not eat, and no better if we do" (1 Corinthians 8:8, paraphrase). In effect, Paul said, there is only one true God. Since there are no other gods, except those made up by the minds of people, faithful Christians can't be accused of idolatry because they buy meat that pagans believe is sacred. As long as Christians didn't join in idol worship they were free to purchase and cook the meat the pagans offered for sale after their sacrifice. This was not a simple "yes" or "no" situation, however, and Paul had more to say.

Although Christians are free, if some of them believed that by buying and eating the meat they would be participating in evil, then it would be wrong and they should refrain. It would not only be a bad idea for them to act against their conscience, it would be a sin. "But the man who has doubts," Paul said, "is condemned if he eats, because his eating is not from faith; and everything that does not come from faith is sin" (Romans 14:23). In this situation two different Christians could participate in the same activity; one would be innocent and the other would be sinning. Paul taught if a Christian believes something is wrong (even if it's not) and he participates against his conscience, he is sinning.

Finally, Paul said Christians should be conscious of how the exercise of their Gospel freedom might affect others who would observe their behavior. Nonbelievers who see Christians buying and eating meat offered to idols might conclude that Christians are hypocrites, lacking spiritual integrity. Paul said others who observe Christians buying the meat might consider their behavior an endorsement of idolatry. Through misunderstanding, a nonbeliever who saw a Christian buy and eat the meat might be encouraged to join in false worship. It isn't enough for Christians to be right, they should also be concerned about how others might interpret their behavior. If someone would be led to sin because he misunderstood the behavior of a Christian, Paul said Christians should voluntarily refrain from exercising their freedom.

Notice that Paul's concern is about weak and new Christians. This is not a situation where long-time Christians were offended by the exercise of Christian freedom causing Paul to urge restraint. When it came to Christians who should know better, Paul had an entirely different approach, challenging them to grow up and accept the truth. (Cf. 1 Corinthians 3:1–4 and Hebrews 6:1–3.)

So should Christians celebrate holidays or only Holy Days? In addition to worship during Advent, Christmas Eve, and Christmas Day, can the faithful allow their children to sit on Santa's lap and leave a carrot for Rudolph the Red Nosed Reindeer? Can Christians celebrate the Reformation on Sunday and take their children out trick-or-treating (even to the parsonage) on October 31st?

The more things change, the more they remain the same. As in Paul's day, there are at least three answers to these questions.

First, Christians live under the freedom of the Gospel. They can participate as long as their actions remain innocent and are done for the pure fun and happiness associated with any secular tradition. To be sure, Christians acknowledge the reality of Satan and should never participate in any pagan rites or activities associated with Halloween. Paul told the Corinthians they could eat the meat but avoid the idolatry. Today he would advise, "Christians can eat the candy if they avoid satanic rituals." Satan is not just a fairy tale made up to scare little children. According to the Bible, he is a fallen angel dedicated to the destruction of Christians. (Cf. Revelation 12:7–12.) He lurks in the shadows, waiting for his chance to entice and then entrap Christians through seemingly innocent occult activities like palm-reading, fortune-telling, Ouija boards, and seances. There is a big difference between trick-or-treating and dabbling in satanic activity.

On the other hand, Christians who believe their participation in these secular activities is a compromise of their Christian faith should avoid them. Paul would state it even more strongly. To violate one's conscience and participate in an activity that a Christian believes to be sinful *is sinful for that Christian.* If Christian parents believe that the world of trick-or-treat, the Easter bunny, and Santa Claus is a compromise of their Christian faith, they must refrain.

Finally, Christians should be concerned about how others might interpret their participation, especially non-Christians and Christians of weak faith. Will others view their participation as hypocritical? Will nonbelievers be drawn into demonic activity because of a Christian's participation in the harmless elements of the holiday? Even though Christians may know certain aspects of these celebrations are innocent, will others who are less knowledgeable be able to make the same distinction and understand a Christian's limited participation?

No doubt many Halloween customs have idolatrous origins but, as Jay Leno observed, most people today care only about the costumes, the candy, and the parties. In most American homes Halloween is a fun night for kids to dress up and ask for candy, nothing more.

Santa Claus and the eggs of Easter also have historic origins lost and forgotten over time. Christian children who participate in the secular customs associated with Christmas and Easter should be taught the significance of their ancient Christian history. To this day St. Nicholas, the Bishop of Myra, (the original Santa Claus—patron saint of Russia, sailors, and children) makes an annual appearance at our congregation's children's service on Christmas Eve to tell the children how Jesus changed his life. They sit in awed silence as the old bishop tells them how, because of Jesus, he gave all his money to help the poor. He concludes with the words, "Saint Nicholas is nothing. Christ is everything. Depart in peace, and ..." (All the children join in the well-known response:) "Serve the Lord!" It has proven an excellent way for us to teach the prominence of Christ over secular practice.

Because these holiday customs have become as much a part of America as eating turkey at Thanksgiving and hanging lights on evergreens at Christmas, Christian participation in most secular traditions has little or no potential to lead others into false worship. But, as Paul taught, it remains an individual decision that may be right for some and wrong for others. This is a case where belief dictates practice—practice that may or may not be contrary to popular belief.

Each Christian family will have to decide their own level of participation based on God's Word and their understanding of the event. The Scripture references regarding Paul's advice to the first century Christians are from Romans 14:13–23, 1 Corinthians 8 and 10:23–33.

As Paul said, "'Everything is permissible'—but not everything is beneficial. 'Everything is permissible'—but not everything is constructive. Nobody should seek his own good, but the good of others" (1 Corinthians 10:23–24). So what are those things that are beneficial, constructive, *and* permissible? In a different letter Paul offered these suggestions: "Whatever is true, whatever is noble, whatever is right, whatever is pure, whatever is lovely, whatever is admirable—if anything is excellent or praiseworthy—think about such things. Whatever you have learned or received or heard from me, or seen in me—put it into practice. And the God of peace will be with you" (Philippians 4:8–9).

CHAPTER SEVEN

Sink or Swim

There is more than one way to drown.

A*If it is possible, as far as it depends on you, live at peace with everyone. Do not take revenge, my friends, but leave room for God's wrath, for it is written: "It is mine to avenge; I will repay," says the Lord." Romans 12:18–19*

laska has been called America's last unspoiled frontier. Its rich forests, raging rivers, majestic coastline, bountiful wildlife, frozen tundra, and natural resources make it a very special part of the United States. No other state is like it. It is also the only state in America where people can become trapped and die in glacial quicksand.

In an article published by *Guideposts* magazine, Jim Ness tells of the relentless effort by an Alaskan rescue team to find a solution to this tragic and recurring nightmare. The search for a solution was heightened by the 1988 senseless death of Adeana Dickison. Adeana was on her honeymoon, walking with her husband along the Alaskan shoreline when she became mired in the silt's deadly grip. Despite hours of frantic effort by fourteen men, Adeana drowned in the rising tide. Jim and other rescue workers across the state listened helplessly over their radios as the silt claimed its latest victim. Bob Hancock, a fellow member of Jim's rescue team, pledged to help find a solution to this senseless killer. Jim's article described the deadly quality of the glacial silt:

Alaskan quicksand, which is as deceptive as it is deadly, can be found in coastal areas. Mud that is often firm enough for walking may become a treacherous trap as the tide rises. Inland, similar dangers lurk under stable-looking peat moss.

This gray glacial silt is formed of grains as fine as talcum powder. If your foot sinks in it, the water flows out and the grains lock around your leg, pulling with as much as 500 pounds of suction. The more you wriggle, the more you sink. Once trapped, there's not a whole lot of hope. One victim was torn in half by a helicopter attempting to lift him from the tenacious muck.[9]

After months of prayer, persistence, and effort, the Alaska Mat-Su Borough Dive Rescue Team hit upon a solution. Using a sealed pipe flared at the end with holes drilled near the bottom, they were able to deliver a high-pressure burst of air deep in the mire, helping break the suction and free the victim. Skim boards helped the team get close enough to accomplish the rescue. Jim credits prayer and persistence with the breakthrough.

Like glacial silt, certain sins are listed in the Bible as especially deadly. Like quicksand, these sins hold their victims in an unrelenting grasp, slowly pulling them under. The deadliest of sins include "sexual immorality, impurity and debauchery; idolatry and witchcraft; hatred, discord, jealousy, fits of rage, selfish ambition, dissension, factions and envy; drunkenness, orgies, and the like." The apostle Paul wrote to the Galatians, "I warn you, as I did before, that those who live like this will not inherit the kingdom of God" (Galatians 5:19–21). The key to their deadly nature is found in Paul's warning, "those who live like this." Perfection is God's requirement for heaven. Fortunately He provides what He demands in the forgiveness every Christian receives by faith in Jesus Christ. But "those who live like this" (as Paul warned) are in effect saying, "For this sin I don't repent, or in this area of my life not even God can help." Everyone sins, but lifestyle sins are different by nature. They slowly drag their victims down into the glacial silt of guilt and shame.

Hatred is on the list as one of the more dangerous sins. Its strong grasp holds great power to destroy the faith of its victims. Friends and family often stand helplessly near, unable to pry the victims from hatred's grasp. Horrified, they watch while their loved ones self-destruct. No counsel seems able to save.

The nature of hatred is no mystery. It is the opposite of love. It is as easy to see as it is hard to overcome. Using Paul's analogy it might take one of these forms:

> Hatred is impatient, hatred is cruel. It results in envy, it readily boasts, and is often proud. It is rude, it is self-seeking, it is easily angered, it keeps meticulous record of wrongs. Hatred delights in evil and rejoices in lies. It always betrays, always doubts, always despairs, always is overcome. Hatred always fails.[10] (Cf. 1 Corinthians 13:4–8.)

Because of hatred's deadly nature, God requires that all Christians forgive others in the same way that God through Christ has forgiven them. In his counsel about love, Paul concludes, "When I was a child, I talked like a child, I thought like a child, I reasoned like a child. When I became a man, I put childish ways behind me" (1 Corinthians 13:11). When I was younger in my faith, I thought forgiveness was for the benefit of the forgiven. I thought like a child. Now I know the greatest benefit of forgiveness is reserved for the one who forgives. Those who cannot forgive continue to suffer the hurt and pain of the past in their present and their future. Like a cancer, it eats away. Like quicksand, it is unrelenting.

The solution to injustice is not revenge. Hatred leads only

to greater sin and an escalation of evil. The only answer is forgiveness, and the power to forgive can only come from Christ. Christians are not to forgive others because they ask for it nor because they deserve it. And forgiving those who wrong you will not necessarily make everything better. Making things better is not the primary reason we forgive.

Christians forgive because they have been forgiven and because it is clearly God's will. The Bible says, "If it is possible, as far as it depends on you, live at peace with everyone. Do not take revenge, my friends, but leave room for God's wrath, for it is written: 'It is mine to avenge; I will repay,' says the Lord. On the contrary: 'If your enemy is hungry, feed him; if he is thirsty, give him something to drink. In doing this, you will heap burning coals on his head.' Do not be overcome by evil, but overcome evil with good" (Romans 12:18–21).

To Jim Ness, Bob Hancock, and the other members of the Alaska Mat-Su Borough Rescue Team, there was nothing more tragic than a young woman drowning on her honeymoon, trapped in a pit of glacial silt. But all around us both the young and the old are drowning in resentments and unresolved anger. Workers who have lost their jobs are being destroyed, not so much by their loss of income but by their loss of perspective. Jilted lovers, abused children, innocent victims, targets of gossip, and victims of injustice are slowly having the life squeezed out of them. When hatred fills a heart there is room for little else, including faith. If God is love (1 John 4:16), then where does hatred come from? Is there any hope?

In the 1970s I was a young seminary student in Springfield, Illinois. During those years the "Battle for the Bible" was raging in my denomination. Not unlike that experienced by other denominations during those times, there was deep disagreement on our college and seminary campuses and among some pastors of our denomination about the true nature of inspiration. Was the Bible *altogether* God's Word and without errors, or did it *only contain* God's Word intermixed with the opinions and prejudices of its human authors?

Elections for leadership positions of our church body were hotly contested. The man elected to the presidency during those years took a firm position on the side of a Bible without errors and untainted by the tenets and prejudices of its human authors. I'm sure he had his hands full. Those were hard years for everyone, but especially for pastors and church leaders as they tried to sort out truth from popular belief. The rumor mills were busy, and my seminary campus was a hotbed of discussion.

In the midst of the controversy most of the students and a majority of the professors at our denomination's St. Louis seminary walked off the campus in a protest against denomination pressure to conform and as a show of solidarity for professors who were being accused of false teaching. A seminary-in-exile (seminex) was established and immediately began to graduate students ready to accept the pulpits of our denomination's congregations.

Would our denomination's leaders allow these self-exiled graduates to be certified for ministry and installed as pastors of our congregations? Where did these new graduates stand on the issues of inspiration and the nature of the Bible? Some district officials in our denomination began to install these seminex graduates in congregations around the country. Being full of myself and knowing all the answers as I thought I did, I took it upon myself to advise the president on the proper course of action.

With the help and encouragement of a like-minded professor, I dashed off a letter urging swift action against those district officials who were ignoring the denominational certification process and installing these questionable graduates. "If the line is not drawn here," I advised, "the tide will turn and your leadership—brilliant and courageous until now—will falter."

The president was not only brilliant and courageous, he was also gracious. He took the time to respond to my letter despite my lowly status as a mere second-year student at the seminary. In what I believe was an act of kindness, he didn't mention or respond in any way to my suggestions. Instead, like a wise father, he reminded me of my immediate task, which was to prepare myself for the high calling I was pursuing. My time, he said, would be better spent studying, not writing letters of advice on topics about which I had very little knowledge. He wished me well and quoted a verse from the first chapter of James, "Everyone should be quick to listen, slow to speak and slow to become angry, for man's anger does not bring about the righteous life that God desires" (James 1:19–20). I have kept his letter as a painful reminder of my arrogance and presumption. I wince a little whenever I think of it, but I also smile as I remember that know-it-all young seminarian.

Later in life, the president and I became good friends, and I was fortunate to travel with him on a number of occasions for the cause of our denomination. Once, when I reminded him of my letter and his response, he smiled politely and said, "Those were the days." I'm sure he had no recollection of the letter, but I have never forgotten it. Every time I read that verse I'm reminded of the contrast between the rashness of my youth and the wisdom of his years. Love, not legalistic demand, is the fulfillment of the law.

Maybe you're caught in the mire of some unfortunate consequence. You've been hurt deeply and your heart is overflowing with bitterness and pain. It is time to sink or swim. An old German proverb says, "The same water that softens the potato hardens the egg." Your difficulty will result in one or the other. Either you will grow bitter and hard or you will grow gentler and wiser. How you respond will determine the outcome.

The world will tell you, "Don't get angry, get even." Your friends may advise, "Give as good as you get! Go down swinging!" Such is the counsel of fools. The right road is the high road. It may seem a difficult, even impossible, climb, but the burden of bitterness can't survive long in the thin air of high elevations. Traveling the low road will only add more pain and grief to your already burdened heart. When you hold on to the resentment, you are giving that circumstance or that person continued control of your life. As if in quicksand, you are stuck in the grasp of the past. Don't let anyone except Jesus exercise continuing control of your heart. It may be contrary to popular belief, but in the end, it is the road to peace.

How can you do it? What's the key? Take Paul's advice: "Bear with each other and forgive whatever grievances you may have against one another. Forgive as the Lord forgave you. And over all these virtues put on love, which binds them all together in perfect unity" (Colossians 3:13–14).

CHAPTER EIGHT

Prayer or Positive Thinking

Is prayer for real?

The prayer of a righteous man is powerful and effective. James 5:16

I t was Henry Ford who said, "Whether you think you can or you think you can't, you're right." Some would say Norman Vincent Peale took Ford's axiom and made a theology out of it. They would be wrong.

There is no question that Peale became a popular spokesman and motivational speaker for all kinds of business enterprises in America. Often in those speeches and seminars he encouraged productivity and effort based on biblical principles without reference to the central teaching of salvation by grace through faith in Jesus. Too few understood his intention. Too many fellow Christians raced to judgment. Whether Peale held views contrary to the Scriptures could be argued, but his position on salvation by grace through faith in Jesus is without question. Peale believed the truth of the Scripture would be recognized and welcomed where the One who gave the truth would never be invited. By sharing the truth, Peale believed those who recognized it would be drawn naturally to the One from whom the truth came.

The turning point for Peale came early in his ministry. Like many promising young pastors, he was asked to offer the dinner invocation for equally promising young executives in New York City. One of his table guests remarked, "This is the closest I've been to a minister in a long time." Peale seized the opening and turned the conversation to a discussion of worship attendance. Those at his table estimated that of the 300 men in attendance only twenty to twenty-five percent worshiped on a regular basis and many of them only because their wives insisted or it was important to their boss. Peale described the moment in his autobiography:

> As I walked home that night, down Fifth Avenue from Fifty-sixth Street to Eleventh Street where I lived at the time, I experienced a powerful surge in my mind. It was like a call. Indeed it was a call, an awakening to an exciting new purpose for my life. I suddenly knew my task was to speak and write and present Jesus Christ and Christianity to the men of our times as the most exciting, practical, tremendous way of life available. If there were men not coming to church in large numbers, I would go to them, everywhere. So help me God, I would dedicate my life to bringing men into a vital Christian life-style in the church if it took me fifty years. Before reaching my apartment, in my mind I had embarked on a one-man crusade to make the businessmen of America realize the dynamic, spiritual, exhilarating fulfillment awaiting them by following Jesus Christ, the most exciting Man Who ever lived and Who still lives.[11]

Peale believed if he could help business people see value in the truth of God's Word, they would naturally want to learn more about the Truth-Giver. What many saw as a compromise of integrity, Peale viewed as an intentional strategy. His commitment to the Gospel was solid. Once, when sitting with Dr. Billy Graham on a platform before a sea of faces at Madison Square Garden, Peale turned to Graham and asked the secret to his popularity. Peale recalled the moment as Graham turned to him with a winsome smile and said, "By practicing the power of positive thinking." Peale commented, "We both laughed, but each of us knew that the real answer was the power of Christ working in him."[12] Peale knew that Christ was the only sure basis for positive expectation.

Christians have every reason to have confidence in life, every reason to be positive people. As the apostle said, "What, then, shall we say in response to this? If God is for us, who can be against us? He who did not spare His own Son, but gave Him up for us all—how will He not also, along with Him, graciously give us all things?" (Romans 8:31–32) Let's not jump to a wrong conclusion based on two verses snatched out of their rightful context. The Lord here is *not* promising a name-it-and-claim-it kind of prayer-power. He *is* assuring Christians that the same God who loved them enough to send His only Son to die for them will provide for their needs according to His wisdom. He *is* telling them that because of Jesus, they can be absolutely positive about God's desire to bless His children.

The love of the Lord for His children does not mean Christians escape all difficulty or receive every request they make in confident faith. In the Garden of Gethsemane, just before His arrest, trial, and ultimate crucifixion, Jesus prayed an earnest and heartfelt prayer contingent upon the will of His Father. Not eager to experience the severe testing and torture that would fall to Him as the world's Passover Lamb, He pleaded, "My Father, if it is possible, may this cup be taken from me." Not willing to violate the will of His Father for the sake of His own safety, He also prayed, "Yet not as I will, but as You will" (Matthew 26:39). We all know the Father's answer to His own Son's prayer. "They stripped Him and put a scarlet robe on Him, and then twisted together a crown of thorns and set it on His head. They put a staff in His right hand and knelt in front of Him and mocked Him. 'Hail, king of the Jews!' they said. They spit on Him, and took the staff and struck Him on the head again and again. After they had mocked Him, they took off the robe and put His own clothes on Him. Then they led Him away to crucify Him" (Matthew 27:28–31). The Father heard His Son's prayer, considered His request, weighed it against the needs of all people and the promises of the prophets, and answered accordingly. Request denied. The prophet's words were fulfilled, "Surely He took up our infirmities and carried our sorrows, yet we considered Him stricken by God, smitten by Him, and afflicted. But He was pierced for our transgressions, He was crushed for our iniquities; the punishment that brought us peace was upon Him, and by His wounds we are healed" (Isaiah 53:4–5).

When our prayer and God's will coincide, great power is unleashed and things change. John told the first century Christians, "This is the confidence we have in approaching God: that if we ask anything according to His will, He hears us. And if we know that He hears us—whatever we ask—we know that we have what we asked of Him" (1 John 5:14–15). Did you notice those four little words again—"according to His will." When our prayer and His will are in sync there is nothing impossible, no need unmet, no sickness incurable. How should we pray? Our attitude should be like the one who prayed,

> Father, we pray, not for everything we want, but for everything we need; not for strength to achieve, but for humility to obey; not for health to do greater things, but for strength to do better things; not for riches that we might be happy, but for the fear of God that we might be wise; not for power that we might have the praise of men, but for devoutness that we might feel the need for God; not for earthly things, that we might enjoy life; but for life that we might pursue heavenly things; Amid life's great

things, let us appreciate the little things; through Jesus
Christ, our Lord. Amen.

How can we know what to pray for, and how to pray? The
Bible has much to say about effective prayer. The Lord's own
prayer and the advice preceding it in Matthew chapter six are
worthy of study.

- If you pray to be noticed, don't expect anything from the
  Lord.
- Sincere private prayers are especially honored by God.
- Long repetitious prayers are of no special value.
- Don't pray to inform God. He knows your needs before
  you ask.
- Six of the seven petitions in the Lord's prayer are about
  spiritual matters: honoring God, extending His kingdom,
  accomplishing His will, forgiveness of sins, help in
  temptation, and protection from evil.
- Only one petition in the Lord's prayer is about temporal
  needs, and like the manna of Israel, each day's need
  should be the extent of your concern.
- If you expect forgiveness from God, you must be forgiving of others.

When our work at St. John's was just beginning, we faced
the challenge of stuffing a growing congregation into a forty-
year-old facility. Every Sunday the windows that separated
our narthex from the main sanctuary were flung open and
folding chairs were arranged in tight rows to make room for
the overflow of people. When the seats were filled, people
stood against the back wall. Members and visitors would
open the door from the street, see the crowd, and leave. Four
different worship opportunities weren't enough to accommo-
date the demand. We had to do something, but the size of our
need and the reach of our resources had little in common.

About that same time the Lord brought to my attention the work of the English missionary J. Hudson Taylor.

J. Hudson Taylor felt God's compulsion to preach Christ throughout China in the mid-1800s. Thousands of miles from home during an age of sailing vessels, without hope of any direct or continuing support, Taylor relied completely on prayer to meet his daily needs. He reasoned, "I shall have no claim on anyone for anything. My only claim will be on God."[13] God did supply his needs, causing more than four thousand of his fellow Englishmen to join in the endeavor which became the China Inland Mission. Tens of thousands in England heard of his work and became supporters. It was all a very humbling experience for Taylor who later reflected, "All God's giants have been weak men, who did great things for God because they reckoned on God being with them. ... We may count on grace for the work, on pecuniary aid, on needful facilities, and on ultimate success. Let us not give Him a partial trust, but daily, hourly, serve Him, 'holding [to] God's faithfulness.' "[14] The lesson was clear—a simple argument from greater to lesser. If by faith Hudson Taylor could begin such a great undertaking, not knowing how God would provide for his most basic needs, then so could we. By comparison our needs and available resources even seemed excessive!

The psalmist wrote, "I lift up my eyes to the hills—where does my help come from? My help comes from the LORD, the Maker of heaven and earth" (Psalm 121:1–2). The one who made the universe has resources at His disposal mere mortals cannot imagine. Having said all that, I want to be careful not to diminish the miracle He was about to work at our church. To build a facility large enough to meet the demands of our ministry for the foreseeable future required the expansion of educational space and the construction of a completely new worship center. The architect's plan called for a $5.3 million project—and that was the scaled-down version! Our annual income was only about $600,000 at the time! Except through prayer and God's provision, how in the world would we ever achieve such a thing?

I began to fast and pray and asked my congregation to do the same. Before we began to solicit any financial pledges or make any final decisions we sensed an overwhelming need for prayer. The leadership of the congregation resolved to canvass the entire congregation for the purpose of prayer. Every family would be visited, receive information about our congregational needs, and be given a cardboard prayer tent (as a reminder to pray) and a Bible study guide on the subject of prayer. In the booklet I outlined fourteen important teachings about prayer.

1. **Be persistent in prayer.**

   Matthew 7:7–11: God expects us to ask.

   Luke 11:5–13: God listens to the persistent.

   1 Thessalonians 5:17: Pray without ceasing.

2. **Set aside regular time for prayer.**

   Daniel 6:10–11: Daniel prayed three times a day.

   Mark 1:35: Jesus prayed before His day began.

3. **Powerful prayer begins with confession.**

   Isaiah 59:1–2: If God seems far away, guess who moved.

   James 5:14–18: Prayer and confession go hand in hand.

4. **Effective prayers are prayers of faith.**

   Hebrews 11:6: Faith provides access to God's favor.

   James 1:5–7: Prayer without faith is best left unsaid.

5. **Don't pray answers—let God decide.**

   Luke 22:42: Jesus prayed to know His Father's will.

   1 John 5:14–15: The Lord answers such prayers.

6. **Effective prayers are offered through Jesus.**

   Galatians 4:6–7: He gives us the right to call God "Father."

John 14:6: Jesus is the only access we have to God's throne of grace.

Romans 8:34 and Hebrews 4:14–16: He stands at God's altar for us.

7. **Find a quiet place to pray.**

Matthew 6:5–8: God loves personal prayer.

Mark 6:46: Jesus often "got away" to pray.

8. **Avoid selfishness in prayer.**

James 4:3: Selfish prayers are ineffective.

John 17:20–21: Jesus' longest prayer was for others.

9. **Prayer is no place for superstition or any notion of good luck.**

Isaiah 44:9–19: There is no power in any object made by man.

Psalm 31:14–15: Only God controls our life.

10. **Effective prayer must be heartfelt but not necessarily long.**

Matthew 6:7–8: God measures prayer by quality not quantity.

1 Samuel 16:7: God looks at the heart not the outward appearance.

11. **Expect help from the Holy Spirit.**

Romans 8:26: The Holy Spirit makes Christian prayer beautiful.

1 Corinthians 2:10–16: The Holy Spirit reveals God's will to God's children.

12. **Blessings are given by God to those who are a blessing to others.**

Luke 6:38: We receive blessings by the standard of our measure.

James 1:22–26: Be a doer and not just a hearer.

13. **Don't seek God's favor with hatred in your heart.**

1 Timothy 2:8: There is no room for dissension in prayer.

1 John 4:19–21: You can't love God and hate your brother.

14. Live by your convictions, avoid hypocrisy.

1 John 3:22: Live to please and He's pleased to give.

John 15:4–5: Our strength is in His power.

Knowing a great deal about prayer is not as useful as being great in prayer. In her excellent book, *The Rebirth of America*, Nancy Leigh DeMoss showed that the greatest leaders of America's past have been people of prayer. I especially valued the observation of S.D. Gordon:

> The greatest thing anyone can do for God and man is pray. It is not the only thing, but it is the chief thing. The great people of the earth are the people who pray. I do not mean those who talk about prayer; nor those who say they believe in prayer; nor yet those who can explain about prayer; but I mean those people who take time to pray.[15]

Prayer changes things. It is the way God's children talk to their heavenly Father. To nonbelievers it seems like useless chatter or mere wishful thinking. But to those who live within the family of God, prayer is a child's heartfelt conversation with his loving, wise, and capable heavenly Father. Earthly fathers encourage such conversations and always respond in a way they believe is best for their children. Jesus said, "If you, then, though you are evil, know how to give good gifts to your children, how much more will your Father in heaven give good gifts to those who ask Him!" (Matthew 7:11)

To be sure, a father's response to his child's request does not always match the expectation of the child. To the child, what's right may seem wrong. But as she matures, the child grows to understand that her father's wisdom is seen not only in the requests he grants but also in the requests he denies. The analogy holds true for requests made through prayer to a Christian's heavenly Father. What's right often takes faith, time, and maturity to appreciate.

As for the building project at St. John's, the Lord blessed those early efforts. The congregation responded with commitments totaling more than $1.5 million. We waited three years until all the pledged funds were received, then asked for and received additional commitments which enabled us to proceed with the building project. Today, St. John's congregation worships in a large, beautiful sanctuary and has a new education wing. Instead of wondering if we were too ambitious, members now wonder if we were ambitious enough. Prayer not only changes situations, it changes people. Everything about that project was contrary to popular opinion but we've discovered that God honors faith over logic and commitment over cash.

CHAPTER NINE

Blessing or Curse

Why doesn't God take better care of us?

M*"For I know the plans I have for you," declares the LORD, "plans to prosper you and not to harm you, plans to give you hope and a future." Jeremiah 29:11*

ost people have no trouble identifying blessings when they see them. A blessing is a good thing and a curse is bad. In a dictionary it looks something like this:

bless-ing (bless'/ing) n. 1. An invocation or benediction; grace. 2. The bestowal of divine favor. 3. That which makes one happy or prosperous.

curse (kur's) n. 1. An appeal for evil or injury to befall another, as through the intercession of God or gods. 2. The evil or injury so invoked. 3. A source of calamity or evil.

In the world of faith things are not always so black and white. Sometimes a curse can be a blessing and a blessing a curse.

Take Joseph in the book of Genesis for instance. Joseph received preferential treatment from his father. The Bible says, "Now Israel loved Joseph more than any of his other sons, because he had been born to him in his old age; and he made a richly ornamented robe for him" (Genesis 37:3). We would say Joseph was blessed. He was the recipient of special favor and was prospered more than his peers. But the Bible also says, "When his brothers saw that their father loved him more than any of them, they hated him and could not speak a kind word to him" (Genesis 37:4). Suddenly things are not so clear. The white is fading toward gray. Was Joseph blessed by his father's favoritism or was it a curse? The question gets even more murky.

Joseph was granted a dream from God. Most would consider a dream sent by God an extraordinary blessing. Remember, "the bestowal of divine favor" is the second definition of a blessing. But when Joseph told his dream to his brothers, they had a different perspective. In his dream Joseph and his brothers were binding sheaves in the field. Joseph's sheaf stood upright and his brothers' sheaves gathered around his and bowed down. The implication was clear and not well received. The Bible says, "Joseph had a dream, and when he told it to his brothers, they hated him all the more" (Genesis 37:5). In his second dream the sun, the moon, and eleven stars bowed down to Joseph. When his father, Jacob, heard this dream, even he rebuked Joseph for his presumption. Was his dream a blessing or a curse from God?

Later, when his brothers were tending their father's flocks far from home, Joseph was sent to inquire about their welfare. When his brothers saw him coming they plotted against him and considered killing the dreamer and his dreams with him. Reuben, the oldest of the brothers, moved by conscience, intervened to spare the dreamer's life. Another brother convinced the others to sell Joseph to a passing band of Ishmaelites. No one would consider Joseph's slavery and all the unfortunate things that he experienced in Egypt a blessing. But through God's intervention, Joseph was rescued from the hatred of his brothers, the injustice of Potiphar, and the prison of Pharaoh to become the second most powerful man in all Egypt. Joseph's dream came true when his brothers came to Egypt in search of grain and bowed out of respect for his office. Joseph's entire family was blessed through his kindness and given good land in Egypt to tend their herds. But later, after his father died, Joseph's brothers feared he would take revenge for their abuse. When Joseph became aware of their fears, he spoke the words for which he is most remembered: "You intended to harm me, but God intended it for good to accomplish what is now being done, the saving of many lives" (Genesis 50:20).

"You intended harm, but God intended it for good." Those words are the secret to understanding the difference between a blessing and a curse in the life of a believer. God is not responsible for evil. In fact, the Bible says, "God cannot be tempted by evil, nor does He tempt anyone; but each one is tempted when, by his own evil desire, he is dragged away and enticed" (James 1:13–14). God made a perfect world. In the Garden of Eden there was no sin and therefore no evil. Adam and Eve never experienced bitterness, jealousy, anger, or resentment until Satan entered the picture.

Today Christians live in a sinful world among sinful people. They are protected by faith, however, and can expect divine deliverance just like Joseph. The Bible says, "We know that in all things God works for the good of those who love Him, who have been called according to His purpose" (Romans 8:28). The passage *doesn't* say that God causes all things. It would be wrong to tell a friend who is grieving over the effects of sin, "I'm sorry, but it was God's will." *Neither does the passage say* that only good things happen to Christians. If that is true, why does the Bible say, "As an example of patience in the face of suffering, take the prophets who spoke in the name of the

Lord" (James 5:10). If the prophets and apostles suffered and even died for their faith, it is wrong to teach that those closest to the Lord experience only good things. *The passage does say* that God can take everything—yes everything: all the evil of Satan, even sickness, injury, injustice, persecution, hatred, pestilence, and death—He can take it all and bring forth good in the lives of Christians who love Him and have been called according to His purpose. What others and Satan meant for evil, He can use for good.

An example of this principle at work can be seen in the life of the King of the Cowboys and the Queen of the West, Roy Rogers and Dale Evans. I can remember sitting every Saturday morning in front of a black-and-white television watching the bad guys lose and the good guys win week after week. Their attitude about life was summed up in the song they sang as they rode into the sunset at the end of every program:

> *Happy trails to you, until we meet again.*
> *Happy trails to you, keep smilin' until then.*
> *Who cares about the clouds when we're together?*
> *Just sing a song and bring the sunny weather.*
> *Happy trails to you till we meet again.*[16]

Little did America know that the King of the Cowboys and the Queen of the West had an ample share of clouds and stormy weather. At the same time they were experiencing such success they were also undergoing trial by fire. On August 26, 1950, Robin Elizabeth Rogers was born. The king and queen were blessed to receive their princess. But all was not well. The doctors recognized almost immediately that something was wrong. Robin was born with a severe degree of Down's Syndrome. Not only was her intellectual development affected, but she suffered severe physical handicaps as well, the worst of which resulted in a malformed heart.

When the diagnosis was confirmed and the severe nature of Robin's birth defects better understood, doctors urged the Rogers to place their daughter in an institutional care facility. They rejected the counsel of the experts, curtailed their travel, hired a nurse, and brought Robin home. The hardship drove them to their knees. Dale recalls praying first that Robin could enjoy a near-normal life, then as the extent of Robin's physical weakness became evident, her parents prayed that God would spare her life. Roy and Dale began to spend hours searching the Scriptures to better understand the nature of God and His ways with people. Instead of anger and bitterness they prayed for understanding. Why was Robin born with such limitations? What purpose was she to serve in their life? The answer came gradually but resulted in a major change of priorities. Roy and Dale decided to become more public about matters that until now they had kept very private. Believing that others were struggling with similar heartaches over birth defects, they decided to talk more openly about their experience and how their faith had helped them cope.

Roy and Dale announced that they would take a moment to speak about the goodness of the Lord and urge their young audience to attend church and Sunday school at every future public appearance. They also resolved to hold benefit concerts for the families of disabled children in every city on the tour. And they would devote their lives to the work of the National Association for Retarded Children (N.A.R.C.). Robin's life became a catalyst for change. The second half of the famous Western couple's life would be lived differently than the first.

Their new mission was not immediately embraced by their associates and staff. In fact, many of their close Christian friends urged them to keep their private life private and their public life professional. Everyone feared all this "Jesus talk" would bring an end to their successful careers. At the time they announced their decision Roy had been the number one Western singer for ten years running. He had starred in 86 movies and his business enterprises were earning $30 million a year![17] Dale was also a star in her own right. She had recorded more than a dozen songs before she married Roy and had toured and appeared in a number of movies. Money, fame, and goodness couldn't spare them from heartache and pain.

In mid-August of 1952, Robin came down with the mumps, in those days a common childhood malady. In her weakened condition, it proved fatal. Weighing only seventeen pounds, her little body and weak heart could not withstand the high fever and after a week of constant care, Robin died. The Rogers buried their precious daughter on the second anniversary of her birth. One month later Roy and Dale were in New York City as the featured attraction for the 1952 World Championship Rodeo. Despite counsel to the contrary, Roy and Dale stuck by their decision. Before his last song, Roy stepped out from the band and addressed the crowd who had filled Madison Square Garden to standing room only.

> "You go to school five days a week to improve your mind and learn how to be a success in the business world," the cowboy king was telling them. "I want you to go to church one day a week to improve your soul and learn how to appreciate it. The most important thing that ever happened to our family was when we started going to church and began practicing what we learned there. The luckiest thing that can ever happen to you is to get to live in a religious home." Then Roy smiled warmly at the children, "Believe me, pardners, it isn't sissy to go to Sunday school. For, don't ever forget a real cowboy needs real faith."[18]

Finishing his introduction, Roy doffed his hat, the spotlights formed a large cross on the arena floor, and in quiet reverence he sang his final song, "Peace in the Valley." Nearby, Trigger bowed in a prescribed show of respect. The king and queen who circled the arena after that performance were treated with a different kind of awe than the Hollywood stars that had entered an hour before. Roy and Dale moved from success to significance and would never go back.

Were they blessed or cursed by the birth of a Down's Syndrome child named Robin? There is no question in their minds. Robin not only transformed their life but through her existence brought about greater reforms in her two short years than many a long and dedicated life has ever achieved. The charity events that the Rogers hosted began to fill with families no longer ashamed or afraid to take their physically and mentally challenged children out in public. America's treatment of orphaned children also began to change as Roy and Dale led by example, adopting special needs children and raising them as their own.

In an appearance Roy made before 50,000 Boy Scouts at a California Jamboree, he spoke of an often overlooked element of success and personal strength. After a prayer on behalf of disabled children everywhere, he said, "I have learned you must help the weak to keep yourself strong. I want you to help them so you will grow strong too."[19]

In the lives of Christians who seek God's will and abide in His love, the Lord turns Satan's evil into good. He changes a curse into a blessing. It may seem wrong, but God's Word is right when it says, "We know that in all things God works for the good of those who love Him, who have been called according to His purpose" (Romans 8:28). Though it is often contrary to popular belief, God's way is always the right way.

CHAPTER TEN

Givers and Takers

God can't be serious about tithing, can He?

D
Give, and it will be given to you. A good measure, pressed down, shaken together and running over, will be poured into your lap. For with the measure you use, it will be measured to you.
Luke 6:38

r. Frank Harrington, pastor of Peachtree Presbyterian Church in Atlanta, Georgia, once told a group of stewardship leaders:

> I have never known a generous person to complain about how much money it takes to run a church. Poor givers gripe about how much it takes. Generous givers express concern that they don't do more.

> I have never known a family who tithed for any length of time who quit.

> I have never known a generous family that was not generally happy.

> I have known a stingy, miserly family that was generally unhappy about many things.

> I have never known a person who was critical of most things, and mad about many things, who was generous.

> I have never found a generous person to be either generally critical or mad.

I have never known a tither who was ashamed of what he gave and who knew it. Almost all stingy people tend to insist on secrecy that covers a multitude of sins.

I have come to believe that most people who feel that we talk too much about money never really want to talk about money at all. Generous people enjoy talking about it.

I have come to believe that there is a direct connection that exists between a person's faith and a person's generosity. Faithful people give generously. Those who give generously tend to become more faithful; and the reverse is true in both instances.[20]

Dr. Harrington has wisely observed and eloquently expressed a simple biblical truth: "Where your treasure is, there your heart will be also" (Matthew 6:21). Those words of Jesus are significant. Notice, He didn't say it the other way around, "Where your heart is, there your treasure will be also." No, Jesus cared about people's treasure because Jesus cared about people. The Creator of people knows how people think. Those things people value they support. Those things people support they value. Those who are invested in the things of God will experience a greater concern for spiritual things than those who have no such investment. *Where your treasure is, there your heart will be also.*

Christian leaders are providing a service to the benefit of both the ministry and the giver when the Lord's counsel is followed. Christian stewardship is about blessing not deprivation. The way people handle their money will have a direct effect on their hearts. When the heart's priorities become spiritual, Christians will enjoy the blessings of the faithful. When those priorities remain material, Christians experience the frustration of the self-serving. There is no correlation between degree of wealth and degree of satisfaction. The faithful poor often enjoy contentment even in their poverty. The non-faithful rich often experience dissatisfaction even in their wealth.

My good friend, Dr. Waldo Werning of The Discipling/ Stewardship Center in Ft. Wayne, Indiana, said it best in an article entitled, "Let It Happen to Me as You Said." Werning wrote, "Givers are winners and takers are losers." Commenting on Werning's observation, Ashley Hale agreed. "Givers are winners for these are the believers in life. The givers are not the fearful, the doubters, nor the complainers. They do not give because the receiver is fully deserving of their largess but because to give is to live, whereas to withhold is to perish. The good news is that to give is to begin truly to live; that to become a giver is to become a winner."[21]

The principle of Christian giving is one of the most clearly taught and yet most neglected of all biblical principles. The Bible is replete with God's counsel, the faithful's example, and promise upon promise related to Christian giving.

- A person's best is to be given to the Lord. (Numbers 18:32, Proverbs 3:9)
- The tithe (ten percent of all income) belongs to God. (Deuteronomy 14:22–29, Matthew 23:23)
- The priests also tithed from the tithe they received. (Numbers 18:26)
- Offering must be of value to those who present it. (Leviticus 22:10, 2 Samuel 24:24)
- Withholding the tithe is equivalent to "robbing God." (Malachi 3:6–18)
- God invited His people to test His promise of blessing. (Malachi 3:10, Luke 6:38)
- God rebukes those things that devour the incomes of the faithful but blows away the abundance of the selfish. (Malachi 3:11, Haggai 1:9)

- Those who excell in faith, teaching, and knowledge are challenged by God to excel also in Christian giving. (2 Corinthians 8:7)
- No one should command giving, but it proves the sincerity of our love. (2 Corinthians 8:8)
- Those who give sparingly will receive sparingly, and those who are generous will be blessed generously by the Lord. (2 Corinthians 9:6)
- God never wants offerings to be given under compulsion or grudgingly. (2 Corinthians 9:7)
- God loves cheerful givers. (2 Corinthians 9:7)
- God resupplies and multiplies the faithful's resources for the purpose of supporting Christian ministry. (2 Corinthians 9:10)

Jesus never hesitated to talk about money and Christian giving. Sixteen of his thirty-eight parables were based on discussions of how people handle their money and possessions. In the Gospels, one out of every ten verses deals directly with the subject of money. The Bible offers 500 verses on prayer, less than 500 verses on faith, but more than 2,000 verses on money and possessions.

Christian giving is one of the most obvious ways Christians show evidence of faith, or lack thereof. It is also one of the most frequent opportunities they have to do so.

In the 1960s, the Kingston Trio sang a song about a thirsty man who stumbled upon a deserted farmstead in the middle of an arid wasteland. If he didn't have water soon he would die. Next to the shack stood a rusty old pump with a leather bag tied to the handle. A weathered note told of a water jar buried nearby to prime the pump and provide the life-giving water. Temptation was strong. Would a thirsty man pour his only water down a dark hole in expectation of receiving more in return? Or would he drink the water, struggle on, and leave nothing for the one who followed? The letter might have said something like this:

> This here pump works just dandy as of June, '32. I cut me a new leather washer that oughta last another five year or so. But that leather washer will plumb dry out and needs priming. 'Neath the white rock I hid a filled bottle of water and corked it tite. It enuf to prime the pump but not iffen ya drink some furst. Pour bout a quarter of the bottle and let her soak a bit. Then pour you the rest steady and slow and pump like crazy and you'll sure enuf git water. The well has never run dry. Have faith. When you git watered up, fill the bottle and cork it again. Bury it where you found it for the next feller.
>
> Signed: Desert Pete
>
> P.S. Don't go drinken the water furst. Prime the pump liken I said and you'll git all you can carry.

The analogy to Christian stewardship is not a perfect one. We don't give in order to receive, but faith in the promises of God and faithful obedience to God's Word will require sacrificial acts that seem illogical and foolhardy. We love because He first loved us. Christians return to the Lord the first and the best of what they possess because *they have already received* grace, forgiveness, and salvation from the Lord and Giver of Life.

Neither does God's faithfulness depend on ours. Paul told Timothy, "If we are faithless, He will remain faithful, for He cannot disown Himself" (2 Timothy 2:13). God is by nature faithful. He will not, however, encourage selfishness by prospering a self-destructive attitude. The Bible does teach that He both blesses and frustrates the giver and the taker respectively. It does not teach that He will disown us for our failure. He remains ready, willing, and able to respond when our frustration drives us to our knees to repent, reassess, and renew our commitment to His priorities. While unfaithfulness in giving may result in significant self-imposed losses, it does not disqualify us from salvation, which comes only by grace through faith in Christ.

Several years ago I wrote a poetic comparison of God's faithfulness to our failure. It is based on the words of David in Psalm 103:10 where we are reminded, "He does not treat us as our sins deserve or repay us according to our iniquities."

If God Were Not Faithful

If God Were Not Faithful ...
the sun would not shine.
the rain would be dry wind,
that blew all the time.

If God Were Not Faithful ...
our family would languish
while we, without hope,
would pray prayers of anguish.

If God Were Not Faithful ...
if Christ had not died,
there would be no forgiveness;
in our sin we'd be tried.

But God Remains Faithful ...
our Lord ne'er forsakes.
unlike His disciples,
He no excuse makes.

Yes, God Remains Faithful
our Lord a true friend.
the penitent find mercy,
and love without end.
                    Amen.

His views may be contrary to popular belief, but my friend Waldo is right, Givers *are* winners and takers *are* losers.

CHAPTER ELEVEN

Greatest
or Least

Power, power, who's got the power?

An argument started among the disciples as to which of them would be the greatest. Jesus, knowing their thoughts, took a little child and had him stand beside Him. Then He said to them, "Whoever welcomes this little child in My name welcomes Me; and whoever welcomes Me welcomes the One who sent Me. For he who is least among you all—he is the greatest." Luke 9:46–48

She was just a ten-year-old child, eager to celebrate her birthday. Anne's world revolved around her cat Moortje, her sister Margot, and her friends Lies, Sanne, and Jopie. Like lots of girls "almost eleven" Anne had a secret crush on a classmate whom, unbeknownst to him, she planned to marry.

Her greatest worries were homework, "moving up" in school, and her growing reputation as an incessant chatterbox. As a cure Mr. Keptor assigned Anne extra compositions on topics with appropriate titles: *A Chatterbox, An Incorrigible Chatterbox,* and *Quack, Quack, Quack, Said Mistress Chatterback!* Anne took it all in stride and won the admiration of her teacher through the cleverness of her essays, the last of which was done completely in poetic verse.

From silliness to sadness, from frivolity to fright, Anne's world was about to change. While she was planning her birthday, Adolf Hitler was planning the invasion of her beloved Holland. Anne knew of Herr Hitler and his hatred of Jews, but it would be safe to say he had no knowledge of her. Anne was only a child, certainly no threat to the likes of the Führer who believed good things come to those strong enough to take them from the weak.

On May 14, 1940, (just twenty-seven days before Anne's eleventh birthday) Hitler decided to take Holland away from the Dutch. The fighting lasted only five days. Holland's strategy of declared neutrality was ignored as German panzers, dive-bombing stukas, and goose-stepping soldiers occupied the land. Hitler had patiently waited since January for the weather to break. When it did, he was ready. Eyewitnesses recall how the cherry blossoms fell like a late spring snow under the onslaught of incessant bombing.

Nazi paratroopers and gliders quickly occupied Holland under the cover of darkness, seizing the country's airports, bridges, and strategic positions with little opposition. The 400,000 Dutch soldiers stationed along the country's borders turned to watch the flash of explosions and the glow of fires rise over their cities. The queen left her beloved Holland, and the prime minister announced the nation's unconditional surrender to a disbelieving and shaken people.

The war for Western Europe was over before its defense could be waged! How could it happen? How did it happen? John Lukacs' essay, "The Dangerous Summer of 1940," describes the entire campaign in one short paragraph.

> On the tenth of May, at dawn—it was a radiant, beautiful morning, cloudless across Europe from the Irish Sea to the Baltic—Hitler flung his armies forward. They were winged carriers of an astonishing drama. Holland fell in five days; Belgium in eighteen. Two days after the Ger-

man drive had begun, the French front was broken. Another eight days, and the Germans reached the Channel. Calais and Boulogne fell. Dunkirk held for just ten days. Most of the British Expeditionary Force barely escaped; all their equipment was lost. Five weeks from the day they had started westward, German regiments were marching down the Champs Elysées. Three more days, and a new French government asked for surrender. Here was a drama of forty days unequaled in the history of war for centuries, even by the brilliant victories of Napoleon.[22]

The outcome was predictable and depressing. Might had vanquished right. Wrong had triumphed and justice had failed. Darkness smothered the land like fog rolling in off the Atlantic, quenching the last glimmer of hope. Freedom was banished as a new and evil empire arose. The poet's despair of a previous war in the previous century seemed justified, fitting. For as in the days of America's Civil War, few believed that good would ever triumph at evil's expense. Similar horrors had caused Longfellow to scoff at the joyous sounds of Christmas. As his own son lay critically wounded the poet wrote:

I heard the bells on Christmas day
Their old familiar carols play,
And wild and sweet the words repeat
Of peace on earth, good will to men.

I thought how, as the day had come,
The belfries of all Christendom,
Had roll'd along th' unbroken song
Of peace on earth, good will to men.

And in despair I bowed my head,
"There is no peace on earth," I said,
"For hate is strong and mocks the song
Of peace on earth, good will to men!"[23]

But just as the world's Savior quietly entered Bethlehem undetected by the occupational army of Rome, now quietly in occupied Holland, an unknown and undetected young girl began a secret journal which would prove more powerful than all the tanks, dive bombers, and storm troopers of Hitler's new reich. Before it was over, Anne, and innocent people like her, would be beaten and destroyed by Hitler's reign of terror. Hitler would learn however that power is no match for truth.

> From heaven the LORD looks down and sees all mankind; from His dwelling place He watches all who live on earth—He who forms the hearts of all, who considers everything they do. No king is saved by the size of his army; no warrior escapes by his great strength. A horse [or a panzer tank] is a vain hope for deliverance; despite all its great strength it cannot save. But the eyes of the LORD are on those who fear Him, on those whose hope is in His unfailing love. (Psalm 33:13–18)

Although Anne's country would succumb to Nazi atrocities, Anne's words would live as a testament to the power of weakness. Unread, her childish scribbles seemed harmless to the soldiers who tossed them to the floor as they dragged the Frank family out of hiding. But as the seed of a mighty cedar lies undetected in the cleft of a giant boulder, her words took root. The tiny seed at first seems insignificant and impotent, but its roots, as fine as baby's hair, slowly infiltrate the boulder until by subtle growth they split the monolith and give birth to a giant tree which towers over the ruin. Slowly, ever so slowly, the strength of Anne's gentle spirit grew until the weakness of her words overwhelmed the ideology of her enemy.

Anneliese Marie Frank was born on June 12, 1929, in Frankfurt-on-the-Main, Germany, where her Jewish family had lived for several generations. Her father had served faithfully in the German army during WW I, but with the rise of the National Socialist Party and the growing popularity of its anti-

Semitic leader, Anne's Jewish father moved his family and business to Amsterdam in 1933. Anne grew to love the Dutch people and led the life of a normal Dutch schoolgirl until the Nazis overran the city in the spring of 1940. The Nazis brought their hatred to Holland. By order of the German high command, Anne and her sister were transferred to an all-Jewish school at the beginning of the fall term in 1941. The following April she was required to sew a bright yellow star on her clothing. Each month brought greater threat and the loss of more freedoms to Jews living in occupied Holland.

Anne's folks tried to make the best of it. As a gift for her thirteenth birthday, Anne was given a diary, which she promptly named Kitty. At first, her entries were typical schoolgirl observations on the likes and dislikes of her schoolmates. She commented, "Writing in a diary is a really strange experience for someone like me. Not only because I've never written anything before, but also because it seems to me that later on neither I nor anyone else will be interested in the musings of a thirteen-year-old schoolgirl. Oh well, it doesn't matter. I feel like writing, and I have an even greater need to get all kinds of things off my chest."[24] By the second week, the depth of Anne's heart began to reveal commentary and insights on more ominous subjects.

June 20, 1942: Jews were required to turn in their bicycles; Jews were forbidden to use streetcars; Jews were forbidden to ride in cars, even their own; ... Jews were forbidden to take part in any athletic activity in public; ... Jews were forbidden to visit Christians in their homes; ... .[25]

July 5, 1942: Father began to talk about going into hiding. ... [He said,] "We'll leave of our own accord and not wait to be hauled away." ... He sounded so serious that I felt scared.[26]

The next day Anne's older sister, Margot, was ordered to report the following afternoon for transport to a labor camp in Germany. Early on the morning of July 6, 1942, Otto Heinrich Frank took his family into hiding. Protected by Christian friends, the Franks hid with another family and one other adult for 25 months until their discovery and deportation to the Nazi concentration camps at Auschwitz. Of the eight hide-aways, only Anne's father survived the ordeal. Anne and her sister were separated from their family and transported to the camp at Bergen-Belsen. Witnesses say Anne cared faithfully for her dying sister until the end. Anne also died—of typhus—just a few weeks before liberation by British troops in March 1945.

Anne's father, Otto, was liberated in January of 1945 and made his way back to Amsterdam. Some of the same Christian friends who had helped hide the Frank family preserved Anne's diary until it could be given to her father. He painfully typed her reflections under Anne's own title, *The Secret Annex*. Initially it was distributed just to friends, but the next year it was published. The journal's impact was immediate and enduring, finding a warm reception even in Germany, the nation whose army had inflicted the pain of which Anne wrote. Since that first printing, the diary has been translated into 55 languages and sold more than 25 million copies. Just months before her arrest, Anne wrote of her intention to write a book about her experiences so that her thoughts might endure even long after her death. In the most incredible way, her wish has been granted.

It is not the circumstance of Anne's life that brought notoriety to the young girl's diary; millions shared her suffering. It was the spirit of the young victim whose noble thoughts and optimism burned so strongly that no concentration camp could quench them. Only three weeks before her betrayal and arrest Anne wrote the most powerful observations of her two-year project. Unwavering in hope she wrote,

> I still believe, in spite of everything, that people are truly good at heart. It's utterly impossible for me to build my life on a foundation of chaos, suffering and death. I see the world being slowly transformed into a wilderness, I hear the approaching thunder that, one day, will destroy us too, I feel the suffering of millions. And yet, when I look up at the sky, I somehow feel that everything will change for the better, that this cruelty too shall end, that peace and tranquility will return once more.[27]

The darkness, despite all appearance, had not overcome the light. Like the young girl's refusal to concede to despair, Longfellow's famous poem also reflected his unwillingness to grant evil its due. He went on to write,

Yet pealed the bells more loud and deep:
God is not dead, nor doth He sleep!
The wrong shall fail, the right prevail,
With peace on earth, good will to men![28]

An old proverb says, "God writes straight with crooked lines." The outcome of a godly endeavor may seem predictable enough, but along the way the most optimistic faith is tested by unforeseen difficulty and suffering. The proverb reminds us the road to that eventual outcome contains many an unexpected turn. God is sovereign, but this is not heaven. Three times in the Upper Room, Jesus called Satan the prince of this world. He is a defeated prince, mortally wounded and consigned to eternal death, but until the end he roams the earth like a wounded lion seeking a victim upon which to vent his pain. You may recall, when the devil was thrown out of heaven the angels shouted both good news and bad. Good—"Therefore rejoice, you heavens and you who dwell in them!"

And bad—"But woe to the earth and sea, because the devil has gone down to you! He is filled with fury, because he knows that his time is short" (Revelation 12:12). Until the final judgment, the devil has sufficient power to make life miserable and he delights in doing it.

When ominous black clouds roll, reasonable people look for cover. When an especially violent storm breaks, experienced people brace for the worst. Not always, but sometimes "the worst" becomes reality and the cause appears lost. The battle has been waged but the enemy has won—it's as simple as that. A reasonable person admits defeat, runs up the white flag, and concedes the loss. But God writes straight with crooked lines. The Bible *does not say* He is the cause of all things, but it *does say* He can cause all things to work out for the good of those who love Him and are called according to His purpose (Romans 8:28).

Psalm 37 is the wise counsel of a man who had to endure the crooked lines while awaiting a godly outcome. Young David had been honest, supportive, and faithful to King Saul. The Lord was with David, blessed what he touched, and granted him victory on the battlefield. Through no fault of David, the people began to sing the young soldier's praise. Samuel records what happened.

> When the men were returning home after David had killed the Philistine, the women came out from all the towns of Israel to meet King Saul with singing and dancing, with joyful songs and with tambourines and lutes. As they danced, they sang: "Saul has slain his thousands, and David his tens of thousands."
>
> Saul was very angry; this refrain galled him. "They have credited David with tens of thousands," he thought, "but me with only thousands. What more can he get but the kingdom?" And from that time on Saul kept a jealous eye on David. (1 Samuel 18:6–9)

From that day on Saul sought every opportunity to destroy an innocent man. David looked like the loser. Power and position were in Saul's corner. Despite years of running and rejection, David continued to believe that God controlled the outcome, and he refused to give up hope. He knew that God writes straight with crooked lines. In Psalm 37 David warns godly people to reject the temptation to believe that might equals right or that the end justifies the means.

> Do not fret because of evil men or be envious of those who do wrong; for like the grass they will soon wither, like green plants they will soon die away. Trust in the LORD and do good; dwell in the land and enjoy safe pasture. Delight yourself in the LORD and He will give you the desires of your heart. Commit your way to the LORD; trust in Him and He will do this: He will make your righteousness shine like the dawn, the justice of your cause like the noonday sun. Be still before the LORD and wait patiently for Him; do not fret when men succeed in their ways, when they carry out their wicked schemes. Refrain from anger and turn from wrath; do not fret—it leads only to evil. For evil men will be cut off, but those who hope in the LORD will inherit the land. A little while, and the wicked will be no more; though you look for them, they will not be found. But the meek will inherit the land and enjoy great peace. The wicked plot against the righteous and gnash their teeth at them; but the LORD laughs at the wicked, for He knows their day is coming. The wicked draw the sword and bend the bow to bring down the poor and needy, to slay those whose ways are upright. But their swords will pierce their own hearts, and their bows will be broken. Better the little that the righteous have than the wealth of many wicked; for the power of the wicked will be broken, but the LORD upholds the righteous. The days of the blameless are known to the LORD, and their inheritance will endure forever. (Psalm 37:1–18)

David offers ten reasons to do the right thing without compromising godly integrity, even when it seems apparent that compromise would lead to greater success.

1. Those who do evil will eventually wither like grass. (v. 2)
2. The ultimate outcome is in the hands of the Lord. (v. 4)
3. The Lord will establish and uphold righteous behavior. (v. 6)
4. Anger and resentment lead to more evil. (v. 8)
5. Those who hope in the Lord will receive the ultimate blessing. (v. 9)
6. When an evil person dies he has no posterity. (v. 10)
7. The meek inherit the land and enjoy peace. (v. 11)
8. The plots of the wicked backfire. (vv. 12–15)
9. Having only a little with righteousness is better than wealth with wickedness. (v. 16)
10. The righteous will receive an inheritance which will endure. (v. 18)

David lived what he taught. When tempted to exchange might for right, David refused to do so and would not allow others to exercise illicit power on his behalf. Twice he was given the opportunity to end Saul's unfair treatment and kill the man who had sworn to kill him. But David refused to kill his enemy and would not give permission for others to kill the king on his behalf. Believing that doing right was more important than exercising power, he allowed Saul to escape. When the danger had passed, David revealed himself and called out to Saul:

> This day you have seen with your own eyes how the LORD delivered you into my hands in the cave. Some urged me to kill you, but I spared you; I said, "I will not lift my hand against my master, because he is the LORD's anointed." See, my father, look at this piece of your robe

in my hand! I cut off the corner of your robe but did not kill you. Now understand and recognize that I am not guilty of wrongdoing or rebellion. I have not wronged you, but you are hunting me down to take my life. May the LORD judge between you and me. And may the LORD avenge the wrongs you have done to me, but my hand will not touch you. (1 Samuel 24:10–12)

On another occasion, David snuck into the very center of Saul's camp while his guards slept. David's friend again offered to kill the evil king on David's behalf, but David would not permit it. Instead, David took the king's spear and the water jug next to his head. After crossing the valley to the safety of high ground, David called out:

The LORD rewards every man for his righteousness and faithfulness. The LORD delivered you into my hands today, but I would not lay a hand on the LORD's anointed. As surely as I valued your life today, so may the LORD value my life and deliver me from all trouble. (1 Samuel 26:23–24)

The exercise of power seems the right way to accomplish great things. But as David's son Solomon later wrote, "The race is not to the swift or the battle to the strong, nor does food come to the wise or wealth to the brilliant or favor to the learned; but time and chance happen to them all" (Ecclesiastes 9:11).

The only way to guarantee the outcome of any activity is to know and do the will of God as David did in his ongoing trouble with Saul. He resisted the temptation to take things into his own hands. Centuries later, Paul's advice to the Christians in Rome echoed the simple wisdom of King David.

Do not repay anyone evil for evil. Be careful to do what is right in the eyes of everybody. If it is possible, as far as it depends on you, live at peace with everyone. Do not take revenge, my friends, but leave room for God's wrath, for it is written: "It is mine to avenge; I will repay," says the Lord. On the contrary: "If your enemy is hungry, feed him; if he is thirsty, give him something to drink. In doing this, you will heap burning coals on his head." Do not be overcome by evil, but overcome evil with good. (Romans 12:17–21)

Not even Jesus gained His victory by a show of power or the exercise of divine authority. Our salvation was won when Jesus "made Himself nothing, taking the very nature of a servant, being made in human likeness. And being found in appearance as a man, He humbled Himself and became obedient to death—even death on a cross!" (Philippians 2:7–8)

The Gospel is foolishness, but in the foolishness of God there is power. The Lord honored David's commitment to humility and made him king. The heavenly Father accepted the sacrifice of His only Son, Jesus, and, as Paul explains, "exalted Him to the highest place and gave Him the name that is above every name, that at the name of Jesus every knee should bow, in heaven and on earth and under the earth, and every tongue confess that Jesus Christ is Lord, to the glory of God the Father" (Philippians 2:9–11).

The least are the greatest in the kingdom of God. What's right seems wrong to most, but contrary to popular belief, it is the power of God and the wisdom of God.

CHAPTER TWELVE

A Good Word or God's Word

Do you believe in inspiration?

To the Jews who had believed Him, Jesus said, "If you hold to My teaching, you are really My disciples. Then you will know the truth, and the truth will set you free." John 8:31–32

Truth has an edge to it, and it's razor sharp. I remember how eagerly I looked forward to summer break after my first year at college. My heart overflowed with new ideas which I wanted to share with my "less-educated" family and friends back in the farm belt of Indiana. As a student of theology, I had been privileged to learn the "inside stuff" and was eager to receive the admiration my new-found wisdom would surely engender. James Kennedy's *Evangelism Explosion* was very popular in those days and my home congregation had an active visitation ministry. Though only home for the summer, I took full advantage of the practical experience and was soon making evangelism calls under the supervision of more-experienced trainers. Between calls my trainer and I engaged in lively theological discussions, which provided the perfect opportunity to showcase my sophisticated understanding of Scripture.

I particularly remember an evening when I was assigned to make visits with Bob Young, an enthusiastic witness and great listener. Before the night was over I had crammed an entire semester of higher-critical biblical interpretation into a one-hour, rapid-fire monolog. As best I can remember, we didn't find anyone home that evening, which gave me the perfect opportunity to impress Bob with my explanations of the JEDP sources which I believed were used to write the Pentateuch after the Babylonian captivity.[29] This popular theological theory was an obvious rejection of the simple (and biblical) view that Moses wrote the first five books of the Bible.

When I finally finished what I considered an excellent and precise explanation of the complex subject matter, I paused to receive the praise and awe of the less fortunate. I will never forget Bob's simple but powerful response. "Somehow, Stephen," he said quite calmly, "that just doesn't seem right to me." I remember mumbling something about not explaining it too well and quietly wondered if such discussions were just too complex for someone as simple as Bob. But no matter what defense I raised, Bob's words could not be easily dismissed. Twenty years later, I can still close my eyes and picture the whole conversation. "Somehow, Stephen, that just doesn't seem right to me." What embarrassed me then now makes me smile.

Bob was right and I was wrong. He didn't need a college education to undo my sophisticated thinking. The truth has an edge to it and Christians know it when they hear it. The Bible teaches no one can say "Jesus is Lord" unless the Spirit of God dwells in his or her heart (1 Corinthians 12:3). That same indwelling Spirit convicts believing hearts whenever God's truth is taught. The Word goes forth with power. Paul told the Christians at Rome, "Those who are led by the Spirit of God are sons of God ... The Spirit Himself testifies with our spirit that we are God's children" (Romans 8:14, 16).

Although Christians recognize the truth when they hear it,

that doesn't mean they always accept it. Christians have been known to wage great internal battles against the truth if acceptance would rob them of personal pride or pleasure. The fervor of their defensive posture betrays them. How true the passage that reads, "The word of God is living and active. Sharper than any double-edged sword, it penetrates even to dividing soul and spirit, joints and marrow; it judges the thoughts and attitudes of the heart. Nothing in all creation is hidden from God's sight. Everything is uncovered and laid bare before the eyes of Him to whom we must give account" (Hebrews 4:12–13).

Since the night I rode with Bob, I have never worried much about winning a battle for truth. The Word does its own fighting, as the story of Brother Joe and the Topeka State House vividly demonstrates.

Joe Wright was the senior pastor of Central Christian Church in Wichita, Kansas, when he was asked to offer the prayer at the beginning of the legislative session on January 23, 1996. The legislators got more than they bargained for. In prophetic fashion Brother Joe prayed:

> Heavenly Father, we come before You today to ask Your forgiveness and seek Your direction and guidance. We know Your Word says, "Woe to those who call evil good," but that's exactly what we have done. We have lost our spiritual equilibrium and inverted our values.
>
> We confess that:
>
> We have ridiculed the absolute truth of Your Word and called it moral pluralism;
>
> We have worshipped other gods and called it multiculturalism;
>
> We have endorsed perversion and called it an alternative lifestyle;

We have exploited the poor and called it the lottery;

We have neglected the needy and called it self-preservation;

We have rewarded laziness and called it welfare;

We have killed our unborn and called it choice;

We have shot abortionists and called it justifiable;

We have neglected to discipline our children and called it building self-esteem;

We have abused power and called it political savvy;

We have coveted our neighbor's possessions and called it ambition;

We have polluted the air with profanity and pornography and called it freedom of expression;

We have ridiculed the time-honored values of our forefathers and called it enlightenment.

Search us, O God, and know our hearts today; try us and see if there be some wicked way in us; cleanse us from every sin and set us free.

Guide and bless these men and women who have been sent here by the people of Kansas, and who have been ordained by You, to govern this great state. Grant them Your wisdom to rule and may their decisions direct us to the center of Your will.

I ask it in the name of Your Son, the Living Savior, Jesus Christ, Amen.[30]

Who would have thought an opening prayer would have stirred more emotion in the Kansas State House than any recent legislative action, but that is just what happened. A member of my Friday morning accountability group overheard a news report on what was called, "The ruckus at the State

House." Four liberal legislators took to the podium to severely sanction Pastor Wright for being so wrong. But the more they railed against the prayer, the more attention it received. Pastor Wright's church had trouble answering all the requests for copies of the stinging call to repentance. In an interview Brother Joe remarked, "You know, if they just hadn't gotten so upset, this prayer would never have gotten so much attention."

Cuts hurt—paper cuts, razor cuts, uppercuts, and those not-so-unintentional comments called, "cutting remarks." God's Word cuts even deeper—all the way to our conscience, which squeals out in pain.

There are really only two solutions to the cutting truth of God's Word. We can run (thus limiting our exposure), or we can acknowledge our failure and receive the salve of forgiveness and restoration offered in the Gospel. Once, when Jesus had offended a large number of people with His teaching of truth, the apostle John tells us that many fair-weather followers began to leave Him. Turning to His twelve disciples, Jesus asked, "And will you also leave me?" Peter answered for us all when He said, "Lord, to whom shall we go? You have the words of eternal life" (John 6:68).

The truth often hurts. The Gospel always heals. Like a hot metal scalpel both cuts and sears, so the Word of truth cuts and saves. The Lord who humbles us can raise us again. The counsel of the prophet is still wise: "Come, let us return to the LORD. He has torn us to pieces but He will heal us; He has injured us but He will bind up our wounds. After two days He will revive us; on the third day He will restore us, that we may live in His presence" (Hosea 6:1–2).

CHAPTER THIRTEEN

Discipline or Disaster

Does God take it out on our children?

I, the LORD your God, am a jealous God, punishing the children for the sin of the fathers to the third and fourth generation of those who hate Me, but showing love to a thousand generations of those who love Me and keep My commandments.
Exodus 20:5–6

This passage is especially well known to Lutheran Christians. Most of us were taught as children to memorize it as part of Dr. Martin Luther's explanation of the Ten Commandments written in 1529. He called it "The Close of the Commandments" and explained it by writing,

> What does this mean? God threatens to punish all who break these commandments. Therefore, we should fear His wrath and not do anything against them. But He promises grace and every blessing to all who keep these commandments. Therefore, we should also love and trust in Him and gladly do what He commands.[31]

Did you notice Dr. Luther did not say anything about children being punished for the sins of their parents? The Scripture quotation at the beginning of this discussion is from the New International Version, normally a very reliable translation of the Bible, but on this passage the scholars missed the boat. Children are not punished for the sins of their parents. The sins of the parents *often become the sins of the children* who are subsequently judged for their own disobedience. It was against the law of Moses to punish children for the sins of their parents, as the Pentateuch explains, "Fathers shall not be put to death for their children, nor children put to death for their fathers; each is to die for his own sin" (Deuteronomy 24:16).

In this instance, the King James Version translates the passage more accurately: "I the Lord thy God am a jealous God, *visiting the iniquity of the fathers upon the children* unto the third and fourth generation of them that hate Me; And shewing mercy unto thousands of them that love Me, and keep My commandments" (Exodus 20:5–6 KJV, emphasis added).

It is logical to assume that the attitudes and abuses of one generation are passed on to the next. The Hebrew word *paw-kad* is used to describe how the Lord *visits* the sins that the fathers have passed on to their children. Those who hate the Lord and all He stands for pass those attitudes to their children who in turn suffer judgment because their parents (not God) caused them to reject the Lord, their only hope of salvation.

Families have great influence on the spiritual development of children. A colleague of mine used this illustration:

The Wayward Sheep

'Twas a sheep, not a lamb, that strayed away,
In the parable Jesus told—
A grown-up sheep that had gone astray
From the ninety and nine in the fold.

Out in the meadows, out in the cold,
'Twas a sheep the good shepherd sought,
And back in the flock, safe into the fold,
'Twas a sheep the good shepherd brought.

And why for the sheep should we earnestly long,
And as earnestly hope and pray?
Because there's a danger, if they go wrong,
They will lead the young lambs astray.

For the lambs will follow the sheep, you know.
Wherever the sheep may stray:
If the sheep go wrong, it will not be long
'Til the lambs are as wrong as they.

And so with the sheep we earnestly plead,
For the sake of the lambs today:
If the lambs are lost, what a terrible cost
Some sheep will have to pay.
Author Unknown

At one time everyone knew the Lord. Today there are more of God's sheep walking the broad road to destruction than the narrow road that leads to eternal life. Why? Somewhere in time a sheep went astray and the lambs followed. Now, generations later, entire flocks are wandering outside the care of the Good Shepherd.

Jesus said, "Things that cause people to sin are bound to come, but woe to that person through whom they come. It would be better for him to be thrown into the sea with a millstone tied around his neck than for him to cause one of these little ones to sin. So watch yourselves" (Luke 17:1–3).

Fortunately, parental influence can also result in children being recipients of the love God shows to "a thousand generations of those who love Me and keep My commandments" (Exodus 20:6).

Incredibly, each generation thinks itself quite free from the one that has gone before. Each idea, they believe, is uniquely their own, every inclination new, and each thought original.

Such thinking is not only naive, it stands in direct opposition to the Word. "What has been will be again, what has been done will be done again; there is nothing new under the sun. Is there anything of which one can say, 'Look! This is something new'? It was here already, long ago; it was here before our time. There is no remembrance of men of old, and even those who are yet to come will not be remembered by those who follow" (Ecclesiastes 1:9–11).

The link between the soul of a child and the spiritual condition of the home is stronger than most suppose—an influence for good or evil. Several years ago I wrote a poem describing this unseen but powerful tie.

Parental Reflection

(A Child's Soul)

Today we lead, we chart the way.
Our children trust in what we say.
As young from the nest, each day they go.
At first, not far, within our sight,
But soon beyond, they take their flight.

Tomorrow they will blaze the trail.
Their spouse will help them hoist a sail.
And off they'll go along life's way.
It will seem all new, as though never done,
But the past lives on in the course they run.

The past lies deep within our soul.
Its memories lost, but it holds control
Of the way we think and the dreams we dream.
The twig we bend will that way grow.
It's important work—a child's soul.

Moses was right when he said children live under the sway of parental blunders and/or the benefit of parental wisdom for generations to come. God neither punishes nor blesses children for the behavior of their parents, but the influence of parents is the single greatest determiner of the faith and values of their children.

No generation is isolated from the next. Newton's Second Law of Motion applies: A body, acted upon by a force, experiences an acceleration in the direction of the force and proportional in the amount to it. God-willing, that force will accelerate the movement of the next generation in the direction of the Lord.

CHAPTER FOURTEEN

Good Man or God-Man

Who was Jesus anyway?

Your attitude should be the same as that of Christ Jesus: Who, being in very nature God, did not consider equality with God something to be grasped, but made Himself nothing, taking the very nature of a servant, being made in human likeness. And being found in appearance as a man, He humbled Himself and became obedient to death—even death on a cross! (Philippians 2:5–8)

A simple letter, written by a young girl in 1897, has become an integral part of America's Christmas tradition. Her name was Virginia O'Hanlon and she addressed her letter to the editor of *The New York Sun* newspaper. His name was Francis P. Church, and to this day he is remembered more for his answer to Virginia than any of the more important stories he surely covered in his journalism career.

Virginia's letter was simple. She wrote, "I am 8 years old. Some of my friends say there is no Santa Claus. Papa says, 'If you see it in *The Sun* it's so.' Please tell me, Is there a Santa Claus?"

Mr. Church wrote his classic answer which began,

Virginia, your little friends are wrong. They have been affected by the skepticism of a skeptical age. They do not believe except they see. They think that nothing can be which is not comprehensible by their little minds. All minds, Virginia, whether they be men's or children's, are little. In this great universe of ours, man is a mere insect, or ant, in his intellect, as compared with the boundless world about him, as measured by the intelligence capable of grasping the whole of truth and knowledge. Yes, Virginia, there is a Santa Claus.

Today the world has no difficulty believing in Santa Claus. Public parks proclaim his existence in brilliant displays of blinking lights which cars line up for miles to see. Every year dramatic stories of his appearing are enacted on our televisions and movie screens. Each concludes in a way that reinforces his mystery and supplies tangible evidence of his existence. Colorful books intrigue our children with stories of his exploits, fully illustrated with pop-up chimneys and elves busily working in his workshop. Songs describe how his reindeer dash from rooftop to rooftop or fly with blinking noses on foggy Christmas Eves. Today we have no trouble believing in Santa Claus.

A modern-day version of Virginia's letter might sound quite a bit different than the one written a hundred years ago. She might write, "Mr. Editor, I am 8 years old. Some of my friends say there is no Christ Child. Papa says, 'If you see it in the Bible it's true.' Please tell me the truth, did God really become a little baby? Was Jesus really born in a stable in Bethlehem so long, long ago?"

A Christian editor would surely respond, Virginia, your little friends are wrong. They have been affected by the skepticism of a skeptical age. They do not believe except they see. They think that nothing can be which cannot be comprehended by their little minds. And all minds, Virginia, whether adults' or children's, are little.

Yes, Virginia, God became man on Christmas Day. There is a Christ Child, and He was born in a cow stall in Bethlehem long, long ago. As surely as the stars shine in the night sky and the sun, moon, and earth know their course, there is a God who watches over you and me. Why should it bother us that we do not understand how God could become man and live among us? There is much we do not understand, nor can we explain, and yet we believe.

Who can explain how butterflies, swallows, and wild geese know the season of their migration—winging their way thousands of miles home each year? Our minds cannot comprehend it, yet we believe.

How can millions of snowflakes fall and no two be found alike? It is not only possible, it is commonplace. How can two living cells combine, divide, and multiply in such an intricate fashion as to create a living person? No scientist can mix and stir his elements in such a way as to create what God brings forth from the love of a man and woman. Ocean salmon return to the exact river where they were spawned to lay their eggs. Sea turtles locate the exact beach where they were hatched to lay their eggs and give life to their young.

So you see, Virginia, miracles are all around us. And we are obliged to accept what we cannot explain. How can God become man? The Bible says the Holy Spirit came upon Mary and the power of the Most High God overshadowed her so that the Child born to her was the Son of God.

No Christ Child? How else can anyone explain the martyr's death, the sacrifice of missionaries, and the love of Christians for those who despise and mock them? No Christ Child? Why didn't the enemies of Christ produce His bones and discredit His resurrection? Where did the timid disciples, who hid behind locked doors, find the courage to proclaim His name to the ends of the earth? And why, after 2,000 years, does the whole world stop to acknowledge His birth? No other birth of a king, emperor, pope, or world explorer is so widely honored.

No Christ Child? Who can explain how intricate prophecies foretold details of His birth, His life, and His death thousands of years before they occurred? The ancients said He would come out of Egypt,[32] out of Galilee,[33] and be born in Bethlehem.[34] Who could imagine how those seemingly contradictory predictions would be fulfilled as a young couple journeyed to Bethlehem out of Nazareth (a town of Galilee) to give birth to their Son, Jesus. Even ruthless King Herod unwittingly played a part in the ancient plan as he put toddlers to the sword in a vain attempt to kill the newborn King. As foretold, Herod's atrocity was cause for "Rachel [buried near Bethlehem], to weep for her children," as she had when Jeremiah watched them as they were carried off to the captivity of Babylon through Ramah.[35] Because of the king's evil plot, God warned Joseph in a dream to flee with his family to Egypt until it was safe for their return—safe for the newborn Messiah to "come out of Egypt."

Not even the Lord's people Israel fully understood how all these prophecies could be fulfilled. Philip told Nathaniel, "We have found the one Moses wrote about in the Law, and about whom the prophets also wrote—Jesus of Nazareth, the son of Joseph." Nathaniel, who knew that the Messiah was to be born in Bethlehem and not Nazareth, responded cynically, "Nazareth! Can anything good come from there?" Jesus admired the blunt candor of young Nathaniel and when introduced to him said, "Behold a son of Israel who tells it like it is!"[36] No doubt Nathaniel later had the opportunity to resolve his confusion over the prophecies of Micah and Isaiah and to understand how Jesus could be from Galilee and Bethlehem at the same time.

No Christ? No miracles? How did David look across the centuries and describe the brutal death of crucifixion without ever having witnessed one? In Psalm 22, he described the events of Good Friday as though he were standing on Golgotha. Yet even the greatest skeptic acknowledges that David's writings predated the Lord's arrest, trial, and crucifixion by at least a thousand years. How could he have written, "My God, My God, why have You forsaken Me?"—the very words Christ quoted to describe both what was happening on the cross and to draw attention to David's messianic psalm? How could David have described the mocking, using the very words of the accusers, "He trusts in the LORD; let the LORD rescue Him!"? The suffering David foresaw could only be miraculous as he wrote of Jesus, "My bones are out of joint. ... My strength is dried up like a potsherd, and my tongue sticks to the roof of My mouth. ... a band of evil men has encircled Me, they have pierced My hands and My feet. ... They divide My garments among them and cast lots for My clothing."

No wonder Jesus did not give a simple answer when John the Baptizer sent his disciples to Jesus asking, "Are You the one who was to come, or should we expect someone else?" (Matthew 11:3) Anyone could have said, "Tell John, 'I am.' " Jesus replied, "Go back and report to John what you hear and see: The blind receive sight, the lame walk, those who have leprosy are cured, the deaf hear, the dead are raised, and the good news is preached to the poor. Blessed is the man who does not fall away on account of Me" (Matthew 11:4–6). Jesus did the harder thing. He appealed to the prophecies of Isaiah in chapter thirty-five, "They will see the glory of the LORD, the splendor of our God. ... Then will the eyes of the blind be opened and the ears of the deaf unstopped. Then will the lame leap like a deer, and the mute tongue shout for joy"

(vv. 2, 5–6). No Christ Child? No miracles? The birth, life, and death of Jesus as predicted and accomplished is an account of one miracle after another.

Yes, Virginia, there is a Christ Child. Thank God He lives and He lives forever! A thousand years from now He will still make glad the hearts of Christians, and those who honor His birth will sing His praise in the courts of heaven forevermore.

CHAPTER FIFTEEN

Success
or Failure

Why don't Christians prosper?

The crucible for silver and the furnace for gold,
but man is tested by the praise he receives.
Proverbs 27:21

In my experience, most people manage difficulty better than they manage success. I'm not sure why that's true. I have several theories:

- People have more experience with difficulty.
- Successful people lose their driving purpose.
- Hardship dictates its own action.
- Success requires no urgency.
- Folks are eager to help when you struggle.
- Successful people become self-destructive.
- Successful people rely too heavily on their reputation.

The Bible warns, "Pride goes before destruction, a haughty spirit before a fall. Better to be lowly in spirit and among the oppressed than to share plunder with the proud" (Proverbs 16:18–19). Past success is no guarantee of a bright future. In fact, the passage suggests that previous success may be an obstacle to continued achievement. The New Testament corollary confirms the point, "If you think you are standing firm, be careful that you don't fall!" (1 Corinthians 10:12)

Consider, for example, these observations taken from evaluations of U.S. Army officers. Each had experienced a degree of personal success, but the reviewers didn't offer much hope for future success.

- "I have never in my life seen an officer who can work so hard, and get less done."
- "Can express a sentence in two paragraphs anytime."
- "Honest, faithful, trustworthy, and stupid."
- "He is a frank and offensive officer."
- "Repeatedly has, with muddleheaded abandon, impetuously entangled himself, beyond his authority, knowledge, or experience, into untenable positions, then vociferously waited for extrication."
- "This officer has never made the same mistake twice; however, I think he has made every conceivable mistake once."
- "This officer fails to meet the low standards he sets for himself."

and my favorite,

- "The only reason I would follow this officer into combat would be out of sheer curiosity."[37]

Past success is no guarantee of future success. If He wanted, God could make all Christians successful by this world's standards. Have you considered the extremely difficult job the Lord must have in measuring out blessings upon His children? There is no end to His resources and no limit to His love. The combination of those two elements has destroyed many a wealthy family's children. Their ability to provide for their children without limit often impedes and can even destroy the very ones they want so desperately to help.

I once heard an older gentleman of some means comment on this irony by quoting the old axiom, "Three generations from shirt-sleeve to shirt-sleeve." When I asked what it meant, he explained. "Most who achieve have grandchildren who do not. Our very success," he said sadly, "becomes a detriment to those we love the most."

Have you ever wondered why Christians don't prosper more than nonbelievers? It seems logical to conclude that if God is in control and He is able to do whatever He wants, then His children ought to be the wealthiest, most influential and successful people on earth. Nonbelievers may wonder the same thing. What value is there in being Christian? If our God is God then why do non-Christians often fare so much better? This is not a new question.

Habakkuk pondered the same issue 600 years before the birth of Christ. "Your eyes are too pure to look on evil; You cannot tolerate wrong. Why then do You tolerate the treacherous? Why are You silent while the wicked swallow up those more righteous than themselves?" (Habakkuk 1:13)

The answer he discovered is still the best answer. "Behold, as for the proud one, his soul is not right within him; but the righteous will live by his faith" (Habakkuk 2:4 NASB). First, even though nonbelievers may prosper, the prophet would not envy them because they lacked the greater blessing. Second, he confessed he didn't know what God knew nor did he always understand why God acts in certain ways. He did, however, know that God was kind, faithful, and wise, and, therefore, trustworthy. Habakkuk understood that God saw the whole picture while he had a limited and subjective perspective.

Habakkuk had learned to trust the Lord even when things seemed wrong. The prophet concluded, "Though the fig tree does not bud and there are no grapes on the vines, though the olive crop fails and the fields produce no food, though there are no sheep in the pen and no cattle in the stalls, yet I will rejoice in the LORD, I will be joyful in God my Savior" (Habakkuk 3:17–18). Our salvation is more important to the Lord than our wealth, our health, and yes, even our happiness. He will do whatever it takes to keep our saving faith intact.

Clearly the Bible teaches that God has the power to make or break anyone. A thousand years before the birth of Jesus, King David said, "Yours, O LORD, is the greatness and the power and the glory and the majesty and the splendor, for everything in heaven and earth is Yours. Yours, O LORD, is the kingdom; You are exalted as head over all. Wealth and honor come from You; You are the ruler of all things. *In your hands are strength and power to exalt and give strength to all*" (1 Chronicles 29:11–12, emphasis added). If it all belongs to God and if "wealth and honor come from Him," then why are there so many poor and lowly Christians?

God knows we handle hardship better than blessing. He simply cares too much to bless us beyond our ability to manage. Just before the children of Israel entered the Promised Land, the Lord promised to bless their efforts—but slowly. "The LORD your God will drive out those nations before you, little by little. You will not be allowed to eliminate them all at once, or the wild animals will multiply around you" (Deuteronomy 7:22). The Lord provides what we need to the degree we can manage it. Like the Last Will and Testament I have written for my sons, the Lord has been careful not to dump a lump-sum benefit on people too young (in the faith) to absorb the blessing.

Of course potential for destruction is not the only reason that Christians do without. There are other valid and biblical reasons why God must restrain from blessing those He loves, some having to do with opportunity for witness and others the development of our spiritual and emotional character. The

Lord is motivated by love and our best interest. He knows that too-much-too-soon can be destructive. Remember Jesus said, "My kingdom is not of this world" (John 18:36). Even if there were no heaven and no hell, and this life was the only life we'd ever know, I still don't think God would bless Christians without a good deal of self-restraint. Our culture is wrong to equate wealth, power, and influence with happiness. Some of the most miserable people you will ever meet have money to burn and some of the happiest have never owned their own home.

Isaiah said, "Come, all you who are thirsty, come to the waters; and you who have no money, come, buy and eat! Come, buy wine and milk without money and without cost. Why spend money on what is not bread, and your labor on what does not satisfy? Listen, listen to Me, and eat what is good, and your soul will delight in the richest of fare. Give ear and come to Me; hear Me, that your soul may live" (Isaiah 55:1–3). God doesn't measure success by our standards.

When the RMS Titanic, the greatest ship ever built, began its maiden voyage across the Atlantic on April 10, 1912, some of the world's wealthiest people were on board. The first-class passengers' net worth was estimated to exceed $500 million. They had paid good money for the honor of being first to enjoy a cross-Atlantic voyage in luxury equivalent to a five-star hotel.

The central ballroom featured a sweeping staircase supported by carved hardwood pillars. Passengers could swim in the first swimming pool ever built on a ship, enjoy a Turkish bath, or ride one of the modern elevators from deck to deck. The ship was as long as three football fields and as tall as an eleven-story office building. Unfortunately, its builders had spent their money on the wrong things—things which were ultimately not the most important for their passengers.

There were simply not enough lifeboats for the 2,200 passengers and crew. All counted, there were 1,000 more people on ship than there were seats in lifeboats. Since the ship was believed unsinkable, lifeboats were not considered a necessity. The Titanic sank at 2:40 a.m. on April 15, 1912. An iceberg tore a 300-foot gash along the starboard side just below the waterline. Although it took two and a half hours to sink, hundreds of lives were lost because the unthinkable happened to the unsuspecting. The proud Titanic with all its finery now rests encumbered by barnacles on the ocean floor, 2½ miles below the surface.

As the prophet said, "Pride goes before destruction, a haughty spirit before a fall" (Proverbs 16:18). Success makes us vulnerable to failure.

Jesus achieved greatness through humility and sacrifice. The apostle Paul described it in his letter to the church at Philippi: "Your attitude should be the same as that of Christ Jesus: Who, being in very nature God, did not consider equality with God something to be grasped, but made Himself nothing. ... Therefore God exalted Him to the highest place and gave Him the name that is above every name" (Philippians 2:5–7, 9). It is sacrifice not success for which Jesus is honored.

It may be contrary to popular belief, but at the pinnacle of our success, we are also nearest our demise. For good reason God shows wisdom through self-restraint in blessing those He loves with this world's treasures. "If you think you are standing firm, be careful that you don't fall!" (1 Corinthians 10:12)

CHAPTER SIXTEEN

Life or Death

What happens when people die?

If we are thrown into the blazing furnace, the God we serve is able to save us from it, and He will rescue us from your hand, O king. But even if He does not, we want you to know, O king, that we will not serve your gods or worship the image of gold you have set up. Daniel 3:17–18

It was January 1956. Headlines carried the news around the world, "Five Men Missing in Auca Territory." Depending on your perspective, that news bulletin heralded great tragedy or great triumph. Within days, the bodies of all five missing missionaries would be recovered. They had been speared to death by the very people they were trying to help, a fierce Stone-Age tribe of Ecuadorian Indians.

I first heard of the Faithful Five's bravery in a speech which Jim Elliot's widow made to an auditorium full of college students. She was challenging Christian youth to offer their lives as a living sacrifice to Jesus.[38] There was no bitterness in her tone, no sense of deep regret or longing for what might have been. Instead, Elisabeth Elliot still talks of those days in glowing terms, as something to be honored, remembered, and celebrated. Some would see it as a tragic end. For those five, and for the Auca people, it was the dawning of a glorious new day.

At the age of twenty-seven Elisabeth Elliot became a widow, as did three other young wives with very young children. How could such an account be anything but tragic? The answer is simple. They had already died. They stood with the apostle who wrote, "I have been crucified with Christ and I no longer live, but Christ lives in me. The life I live in the body, I live by faith in the Son of God, who loved me and gave Himself for me" (Galatians 2:20).

Elisabeth's explanation is not the musing of a widow trying to immortalize her fallen husband. The Faithful Five had clearly documented their life's philosophy before that fateful day. Jim had maintained a personal journal even before the Lord called him to mission work in Ecuador. In perhaps the most famous of his reflections, Jim wrote, "He is no fool to exchange what he cannot keep to gain what he cannot lose."[39] He was prepared to exchange life for life eternal.

The violent reputation of the Auca people was well documented, not only against the white missionaries, but against native tribes as well. Dayuma, a young Auca woman, who escaped after her family was massacred in an Auca family feud, was asked what made the Auca people so fierce. She could only answer, "They are killers. Never, never trust them. They may appear friendly and they will turn around and kill."[40]

The missionaries knew the risk they were taking before they went to Ecuador. Other tribes, including the famous "head-shrinking" tribe of the Jivaro and their equally violent cousins the Atshuaras of Ecuador, had already been reached, in part by these same men. In her classic work, *Through Gates of Splendor*, Elisabeth Elliot has gathered the letters, journals, and notes of the Faithful Five to tell their story. Nate Saint, the missionary pilot who flew the men into the remote rainforest (also numbered among the victims), explained the motive for their mission.

> As we weigh the future and seek the will of God, does it seem right that we should hazard our lives for just a few savages? As we ask ourselves this question, we realize

that it is not the call of the needy thousands, rather it is the simple intimation of the prophetic Word that there shall be some from every tribe in His presence in the last day and in our hearts we feel that it is pleasing to Him that we should interest ourselves in making an opening into the Auca prison for Christ.[41]

Christians simply don't think of death in the same way as non-Christians. In life or death the Christian desires to serve Jesus. As the apostle wrote, "For to me, to live is Christ and to die is gain. If I am to go on living in the body, this will mean fruitful labor for me. Yet what shall I choose? I do not know! I am torn between the two: I desire to depart and be with Christ, which is better by far" (Philippians 1:21–23).

I like the way Jesus described death and dying to His dear friends at Bethany. When Lazarus first became ill, his sisters had urged the Lord's hasty return. Christ delayed and Lazarus died. When Jesus finally appeared, Mary remained in the house, unable to face the Lord with her feelings. Martha was not the reluctant type. John records the encounter:

> "Lord," Martha said to Jesus, "If You had been here, my brother would not have died. But I know that even now God will give You whatever You ask." Jesus said to her, "Your brother will rise again." Martha answered, "I know he will rise again in the resurrection at the last day." Jesus said to her, "I am the resurrection and the life. He who believes in Me will live, even though he dies; and whoever lives and believes in Me will never die. Do you believe this?" "Yes, Lord," she told Him, "I believe that You are the Christ, the Son of God, who was to come into the world." (John 11:21–27)

For the longest time, the words of Jesus, although well known and often quoted, baffled me. How can He say one moment, "_____ will live, even if he dies," and in the next breath say, "whoever believes in me will never die."

Which is it? Will he live even if he dies or will he never die? The answer is *both*. Both statements are correct. To those who go on living (people like Martha), Jesus says, "Your brother looks dead, but he still lives." To those who die (people like Lazarus), Jesus says, "There is no such thing as death." Lazarus simply went from life to life eternal.

The congregation that Carol and I serve in St. Louis County recently offered special pricing on grave plots located on "God's little acre" at the southwest corner of our church property. The Cemetery Association was about to raise the price on burial sites but offered members the old rate of $125 for three more months. (The price was so good the principal of our school offered to buy ten lots and build a small home there! When they told him it would have to be below ground and without windows he withdrew his offer.) Carol and I had completed our estate plan but had made no burial provisions, so the timing seemed right.

When I first became a pastor at St. John's eight years ago, I had asked one of the older members if there were any pastors buried in the cemetery. He replied with a twinkle, "No, not yet. We killed a few, but their families always buried them somewhere else!" Never one to scare easily, Carol and I bought two lots at the bargain rate. I again reminded her of the poem I want bronzed and attached to my headstone. It's been in my files a long time and I've often shared it with families who've suffered the death of a Christian loved one. I have never read anything that expresses the Christian perspective on death any better.

The Other Side

This isn't death, it's glory!
It isn't dark, it's light;
It isn't stumbling, groping,
Or even faith—it's sight.

This isn't grief, it's having
My last tear wiped away.
It's sunrise in the morning
Of my eternal day!

It isn't even praying,
It's speaking face to face.
It's listening, and it's glimpsing
The wonders of His grace.

This is the end of pleading
For strength to bear my pain;
Not even pain's dark memory
Will ever live again.

How did I bear the earth life
Before I came up higher,
Before my soul was granted
Its every deep desire?

Before I knew this rapture
Of meeting face to face
The One who sought me, saved me,
And kept me by His grace!
Martha Snell Nicholson[42]

I'm not suggesting that Christians don't grieve. When you have been "one flesh" with a faithful spouse for half a century, or held a baby in your arms that now lies lifeless in a satin-lined box, there is going to be a deep sense of loss. The Bible never says Christians don't grieve. It simply says, we do not "… grieve like the rest of men, who have no hope. We believe that Jesus died and rose again and so we believe that God will bring with Jesus those who have fallen asleep in Him" (1 Thessalonians 4:13–14).

Once a Christian's life is secure in Jesus, it is secure. Once you have died to sin and have been born again in Christ there is no reason to fear death. As Jesus said, "I give them eternal life, and they shall never perish; no one can snatch them out of my hand. My Father, who has given them to Me, is greater than all; no one can snatch them out of My Father's hand" (John 10:28–29). The greatest tragedy is not death, but life without Christ. "Do not be afraid of those who kill the body but cannot kill the soul. Rather, be afraid of the One who can destroy both soul and body in hell. ... Whoever finds his life will lose it, and whoever loses his life for My sake will find it" (Matthew 10:28, 39).

Faith in the promises of God is the only way to explain a Christian's confidence in the face of death. Without faith, death remains the most dreaded enemy known to the human race. Ed McCully, one of the Faithful Five martyred by the Auca Indians, was survived by a young wife, two young sons, and a baby yet to be born. Shortly after his father's death, three-year-old Stevie told his mom, "I know my daddy is with Jesus, but I miss him and I wish he would just come down and play with me once in a while." Several weeks later, back in the States, Stevie's little brother Matthew was born. One day the baby was crying and Stevie offered brotherly comfort, "Never you mind; when we get to heaven I'll show you which one is our daddy."[43]

Stevie had no way of knowing, but shortly before his father's death the Faithful Five had sung of that reality. "We Rest on Thee," one of their favorite hymns, was sung as part of their morning devotional. The final stanza proved prophetic.

We rest on Thee, our Shield and our Defender,
Thine is the battle, Thine shall be the praise

When passing through the gates of pearly splendor
Victors, we rest with Thee through endless days.[44]

It has been said the Church is planted by sacrifice and nurtured on the blood of the martyrs. In heaven the Faithful Five and all the martyrs await their vindication and the ultimate day of glory for Jesus their Savior. John saw them there, under the altar of the Lord. He wrote about it in Revelation. "They called out in a loud voice, 'How long, Sovereign Lord, holy and true, until You judge the inhabitants of the earth and avenge our blood?' Then each of them was given a white robe, and they were told to wait a little longer, until the number of their fellow servants and brothers who were to be killed as they had been was completed" (Revelation 6:10–11).

The wait is shorter today than it was January 8, 1956. It could be any day.

CHAPTER SEVENTEEN

Pitiful or Perfect

Are Christians sinners or saints?

Be perfect, therefore, as your heavenly Father is perfect. Matthew 5:48

A few years ago Tom Wolfe wrote a best-selling book called *The Right Stuff.* They even made a movie out of it. Wolfe's book is about an era some have called the "golden age" of flying. His book recounts the tragedies and triumphs of jet test pilots and the first astronauts. When you think of the "right stuff," the name Chuck Yeager comes to mind.

At the age of twenty-one, Yeager became the first ace-in-a-day, shooting down five German fighters as he escorted bombers over the English Channel. He once shot down a Messerschmitt jet with a prop-driven P-51 Mustang. (The Messerschmitts had a 150 mph speed advantage over the Mustangs but, as Yeager proved, even jets could be caught with the help of a steep all-out dive!) Despite being shot down over occupied France, Yeager escaped to fly and fight again. He emphatically refused to be sent home until after the fighting was over. His stellar war record would have been enough for most, but Yeager wasn't done—far from it. He would make his mark as the greatest test pilot of all time. General Chuck Yeager was one of a very select group who risked their lives to ride experimental jets that were little more than bullets with wings. He was the first man to fly faster than the speed of sound and one of only a few who survived the experimental age of jets and lived to retire. Did he have the right stuff?

"The question annoys me," Yeager responds, "because it implies that a guy who has 'the right stuff' was born that way. I was born with unusually good eyes and coordination. I was mechanically oriented, understood machines easily. My nature was to stay cool in tight spots. Is that 'the right stuff'? All I know is I worked my tail off to learn how to fly, and worked hard at it all the way. And in the end, the one big reason why I was better than average as a pilot was because I flew more than anybody else. If there is such a thing as 'the right stuff' in piloting, then it is experience. ... The best pilots fly more than the others; that's why they're the best."[45]

Why do some make it and others not? What does it really take to succeed? "The secret to my success," said Yeager, "was that somehow I always managed to live to fly another day."[46] In the business of jets there was little room for error, although some pilots walked away from a mistake or two. After the war, Yeager learned that Germany (who had more planes than pilots) instructed their aces to avoid dogfights whenever possible or bail out rather than risk a crash. Some of their leading aces had actually bailed out more than twenty times. In the matter of salvation, there is no room for error—absolutely none.

Salvation requires perfection. The standard of God as Jesus announced it in His sermon on the mount was absolute perfection. "Be perfect, therefore, as your heavenly Father is perfect," is how He put it (Matthew 5:48). It is contrary to popular belief. It certainly doesn't seem possible. How could God require anyone to be perfect? Doing more good than bad—that I could understand, but perfection? Nobody is perfect. Although it defies logic, the Bible doesn't hedge or compromise on the perfection-expectation anywhere in its pages.

In the Old Testament David discussed the subject in Psalm 24, "Who may ascend the hill of the LORD? Who may stand in

His holy place? He who has clean hands and a pure heart, who does not lift up his soul to an idol or swear by what is false. He will receive blessing from the LORD and vindication from God his Savior" (vv. 3–5). No great comfort here. I would be the last to claim clean hands and a pure heart. Perfection will kill you, just ask the experts.

A number of years ago, Dr. David Burns, director of Cognitive and Behavioral Therapies at the University of Pennsylvania Medical Center, published his findings on the destructive effects of perfectionism. He found that rather than increasing productivity and success, perfectionism actually lead to decreases in creativity and success. Perfectionists are plagued by loneliness, depressed over their inability to achieve unrealistic and self-imposed standards, have difficulty maintaining personal relationships, are paralyzed by fear of failing, and, lacking spontaneity, are consistently unwilling to risk new ventures.

Dr. Burns asked a law student who came to him for help to explain what she believed was the advantage of perfectionism. She could list only one, "It sometimes can produce fine work." When asked to consider the disadvantages, the same student quickly listed six:

1. It makes me so uptight I can't produce even adequate work at times.
2. I am often unwilling to risk the mistakes necessary to come up with a creative piece of work.
3. It inhibits me from trying new things.
4. It makes me self-critical and takes the joy out of life.
5. I can't ever relax because I'll always find something that isn't perfect.
6. It makes me intolerant of others.[47]

If perfectionism is so destructive, why do so many live under its grip? It's because we tend to focus on the wrong things. Mistakes, not achievements, receive way too much attention in the average life. Schools designed to help instead often formalize the destructive emphasis on perfection. Teachers are inclined to return papers with misspelled words circled and the number of wrong answers printed in bold red ink at the top of corrected homework. I admire those teachers who make it their practice to write the number of correct answers on the top of student papers and jot at least one positive note on every paper they return to a student. When I taught I always gave my students the opportunity to raise their grade by making false statements true and by copying true statements which they had mistaken for false. In every aspect of correction I tried to find a way to stress what was right, not what was wrong. Graduation from school doesn't necessarily bring an end to perfection-expectation—far from it. The workplace can be just as discouraging.

A business journal I subscribe to contained an article entitled, "Strive for Perfection—OR ELSE!" The article pointed out that if 99.9 percent is good enough then ...

- Two million documents will be lost by the IRS this year.
- 22,000 checks will be deducted from the wrong bank accounts in the next 60 minutes.
- 12 babies will be given to the wrong parents every day.
- 1,314 phone calls will be misplaced by telecommunication services every minute.
- 880,000 credit cards in circulation will have incorrect cardholder information on their magnetic strips.
- 20,000 incorrect drug prescriptions will be written in the next 12 months.
- There will be 315 misspelled entries in Webster's third *New International Dictionary of the English Language.*[48]

Talk about stress! With places like school and work giving

us such pressure to achieve, shouldn't the Christian faith cut us some slack? Isn't God compassionate and understanding? Of course He is, but perfection is still required to gain entrance into heaven. Remember, "Be perfect, therefore, as your heavenly Father is perfect" (Matthew 5:48).

The Lord can't lower His standard. Perfection is His very nature. It is His essence. He is holy, righteous, and just, and as the Bible says, "For what do righteousness and wickedness have in common? Or what fellowship can light have with darkness?" (2 Corinthians 6:14) It's a law of nature: Whenever light enters a room, darkness must leave. The two are incompatible. That's why God, who is holy, cannot coexist with sinners who are not. Whenever He enters the room, sinners must flee; since He is in heaven, it stands to reason sinners like us don't belong there.

If God can't change but He still wants us in heaven, something must be done about our imperfection. He must change sinners into saints. That is precisely what God did when He sent His Son, Jesus. The Lord never lowered the standard. He helped us obtain our requisite perfection through the sacrifice of His Son, Jesus, who was perfect. The Bible puts it this way, "God made Him who had no sin to be sin for us, so that in Him we might become the righteousness of God" (2 Corinthians 5:21). In other words, Jesus took our place, suffered the punishment our sins deserved, so that we might escape punishment. He became a sinner so that we could become saints.

God's solution to man's sin is simple to explain but sometimes difficult to believe. Accepting God's solution to our imperfection requires faith in miracles. The Old Testament prophet described God's plan when he wrote, "But He was pierced for our transgressions, He was crushed for our iniquities; the punishment that brought us peace was upon Him, and by His wounds we are healed. We all, like sheep, have gone astray, each of us has turned to his own way; and the LORD has laid on Him the iniquity of us all" (Isaiah 53:5–6).

Although I am a sinner, I am forgiven. The theologians have a Latin phrase for it, "simul justus, et piccator"—"simultaneously a saint and also a sinner."

Jesus once had a memorable conversation with a young rich man on this very subject. The apostle Matthew was there and recorded the entire conversation in the nineteenth chapter of his gospel. Basically, the young man approached Jesus to apply for sainthood. "I have the right stuff," he said. Jesus asked if the young man had kept all the commandments. "Every one of them," he replied. "What am I lacking?"

It is unclear whether the young man knew instinctively that he was still lacking something or whether he was just baiting Jesus so he might have the opportunity to list all his wonderful achievements. Jesus' answer is insightful and to the point. *"If you want to be perfect*, go, sell your possessions and give to the poor, and you will have treasure in heaven. Then come, follow Me" (Matthew 19:21, emphasis added). With just one well-aimed statement, Jesus uncovered the man's Achilles' heel. Matthew tells us, "He went away sad, because he had great wealth" (Matthew 19:22).

The story doesn't end when the young rich man walks. The disciples who were watching and listening were amazed at the standard of perfection Jesus maintained. If this man was eliminated simply because he wasn't willing to give up everything he had to follow Jesus, then who is good enough? Matthew says the Twelve were greatly astonished at Jesus and asked, "Who then can be saved?" The answer Jesus gave is the answer to our paradox. "Jesus looked at them and said, 'With man this is impossible, but with God all things are possible' " (Matthew 19:26).

What is impossible for man is commonplace for God. The perfection He requires He also provides by grace through faith in the Savior. Though contrary to popular belief, the expectation of perfection is biblical and true. The gift of perfection is the only way sinners can coexist with God who reigns in holiness.

CHAPTER EIGHTEEN

Servant or Leader

Can submissive people lead?

MJesus said, *"You call me 'Teacher' and 'Lord,' and rightly so, for that is what I am. Now that I, your Lord and Teacher, have washed your feet, you also should wash one another's feet." John 13:13–14*

oses had a mess on his hands. Returning from his private conference with the Lord on Mount Sinai, he found the camp in complete chaos. The children of Israel had rejected the Lord, thrown off all constraints, and were "running wild" (Exodus 32:25). Moses took immediate action. Burning the golden calf (the object of their idolatry), he ground it into powder, mixed it with water, and forced the people to drink it. Those who continued in their rebellion were executed—no fewer than three thousand died that day.

Moses was understandably distraught and discouraged. His response to the Lord's marching orders reveals his complete sense of inadequacy:

> You [LORD,] have been telling me, "Lead these people," but You have not let me know whom You will send with me. You have said, "I know you by name and you have found favor with Me." If You are pleased with me, teach me Your ways so I may know You and continue to find favor with You. Remember that this nation is Your people. (Exodus 33:12–13)

Moses' level of frustration had reached a breaking point. What Christian leader hasn't felt like Moses—in over his head and ready to resign? When General John Galvin, the Supreme Commander-in-Chief of all Allied troops in Europe, was asked what it was like to be in charge of so diverse a force, his response was equally revealing. "I often feel like the groundskeeper at Forest Lawn," he said. "I have a lot of people under me, but no one listens!"

The size of the task, although considerable, may not be the Christian leader's greatest stressor. Many Christian leaders serve in ministry traditions that are at odds with the very concept of leadership. They are taught and reminded to be servants. There is nothing wrong with the servant title, but the biblical model of a servant-leader and the modern concept of an ecclesiastical step-and-fetch-it have nothing in common. Many would even object to the term servant-leader. In their way of thinking, a Christian leader simply can't be both at the same time. What's right seems wrong.

As at Sinai, confusion reigns among God's people. Christian leaders are in a quandary over what to do. Their struggle is not unlike the confusion a father-coach has in guiding his daughter's softball team. On the one hand, he knows what strategy is best for the team and has the greatest likelihood of victory. On the other hand, he has to deal with the limitations of his players, which bear no resemblance to their parents' expectations. The syndicated cartoonists Greg Howard and Craig Macintosh did a great job of depicting a coach's struggle in their newspaper strip, "Sally Forth."

Sally Forth

By Greg Howard and Craig MacIntosh

Reprinted with special permission of King Features Syndicate.

How does Ted best serve his team—the players *and* their parents? Who sets the agenda? Fortunately for Christian leaders, the agenda for ministry is set by the Lord. Unfortunately, very few Christian ministries understand and support this concept. Far too many ministries are established and maintained for self-service. Like mothers and fathers screaming for their children, too many members argue for priorities that reflect their self-interest.

A recent gathering of Christian professionals in Missouri was typical of the identity crisis most Christian leaders face. The theme for the conference was appropriately from Psalm 100, "Serve the Lord with Gladness." From the message at the opening service through the plenary sessions and throughout many of the workshops, the theme of servitude was interpreted as subservience to Christ, the Christian congregation, and to one another. No one would argue against the need for complete submission to Christ and an attitude of humility derived from His model (cf. Philippians 2). It is wrong, however, to equate servitude to subservience as the only model for biblically faithful leadership. There is a case to be made for the role of a servant-leader.

As a servant to the Lord and to His people, Moses asserted his leadership. He boldly confronted the reigning confusion and brought an abrupt end to their idolatry. Without asking permission, he assumed authority, ended the revelry, ground the idol into powder, and commanded the destruction of those who opposed the Lord—hardly a spirit of passivity. The biblical history of the Old and New Testaments is largely the legacy of bold servant-leaders.

- Noah endured the hostility and ridicule of those who mocked his faithfulness. No amount of pressure could persuade him to sanction their immorality.
- Abraham left the security of Haran and journeyed to an

unknown land and an unknown future at an advanced age.

- Joseph assumed leadership in a foreign nation for the benefit of all.
- Phinehas, Aaron's grandson, thrust his spear through the back of an immoral Israelite and his Medianite temptress.
- Joshua commanded the attack of Jericho and condemned Achan to death for his compromise of a direct command.
- Gideon tore down his father's altar and the town's idol of Baal.
- David volunteered to fight the Philistine champion and repeatedly led God's people to victory in war.
- Nehemiah was not intimidated by the threats of his enemies and posted armed guards for the protection of those rebuilding the walls of Jerusalem.
- Paul ordered the congregation at Corinth to remove the adulterer from their midst.
- Peter admonished first-century Christians to suffer for Christ as a necessary process in the refinement of faith.

And Jesus (a perfect model of humble obedience to His Father even to the point of death), who also cleared the temple, told Nicodemus (a high-ranking Jewish leader) that he must be born again, compared the Pharisees to whitewashed tombs, and publicly called religious leaders hypocrites. Concerning Jesus, Matthew tells us, "The crowds were amazed at His teaching, because He taught as one who had authority, and not as their teachers of the law" (Matthew 7:28–29). As true man, Jesus served His Father and God's people through the exercise of godly and often bold leadership.

The terms "servant" and "leader" are not mutually exclusive. While not every Christian is called to leadership, all

Christian leaders are expected to demonstrate a spirit of servitude to God and the people He loves. The key to proper exercise of leadership is found in Moses' request: "If You are pleased with me, teach me Your ways so I may know You and continue to find favor with You. Remember that this nation is Your people" (Exodus 33:13). The faithful leader exercises God's authority only when he or she correctly understands and properly pursues His will, for "they are His people."

This is precisely the same counsel given by God to Joshua when He chose him to lead the people after Moses' death. Imagine Joshua's state of mind as he assumed the position of one who saw God face to face! Remember too, Joshua was asked to provide leadership at a critical juncture, just as the Israelites were about to cross the Jordan and begin their conquest of the Promised Land. No wonder God came to him with reassurance and a simple formula for success as a godly servant-leader.

> After the death of Moses the servant of the LORD, the LORD said to Joshua son of Nun, Moses' aide: "Moses my servant is dead. Now then, you and all these people, get ready to cross the Jordan River into the land I am about to give to them—to the Israelites. ... No one will be able to stand up against you all the days of your life. As I was with Moses, so I will be with you; I will never leave you nor forsake you. Be strong and courageous, because you will lead these people to inherit the land I swore to their forefathers to give them. Be strong and very courageous. Be careful to obey all the law my servant Moses gave you; do not turn from it to the right or to the left, that you may be successful wherever you go". (Joshua 1:1–2, 5–7)

The Lord did not tell Joshua to be passive and submissive while remaining faithful to the teachings which he had received from Moses. No, Joshua would serve the Lord and His people best by being strong and courageous in the exercise of God's truth. There are many strong and courageous leaders who compromise God's truth and fall short of the standard for a godly leader. There are many others in Christian leadership positions who remain faithful to the Word but are not strong and courageous in the exercise of their office. There are too few Christian leaders who are strong and courageous and unwilling to turn to the right or left of all that God has commanded.

To be a Christ-like servant is the goal of every Christian leader. Jesus made the subject of servitude a large part of His final instructions to His disciples in the Upper Room the night of His betrayal and arrest. After demonstrating a servant's heart by humbly washing the feet of the Twelve, Jesus talked openly about their relationship with one another and with Him. It was perhaps His most important conversation on the subject of leadership, especially leadership as He envisioned it after His ascension.

> Greater love has no one than this, that he lay down his life for his friends. You are my friends if you do what I command. I no longer call you servants, because a servant does not know his master's business. Instead, I have called you friends, for everything that I learned from my Father I have made known to you. (John 15:13–15)

Jesus makes the distinction between servant and friend—the kind of relationship He was establishing with His disciples. A master has no reason to explain his actions or expectations to a mere servant. The servant or slave is expected to carry out his master's commands without question or need for explanation. Friends, by contrast, establish their relationships on mutual understanding and consent. A servant is bound by law. A friend is bound by love. The latter is the greater bond. Jesus was leaving a legacy of love between friends. It was no longer a relationship of a master to his slaves, but one established on understanding and common purpose.

Shortly before His ascension, Jesus told His followers to make disciples, baptizing and teaching them to obey all that He commanded. He also promised, "You will receive power when the Holy Spirit comes on you; and you will be My witnesses in Jerusalem, and in all Judea and Samaria, and to the ends of the earth" (Acts 1:8). Not unlike the words of the Lord to Joshua centuries before, the Lord was calling them to be servant-leaders, strong, courageous, and unwilling to turn to the right or left of all that the Father had commanded.

Some of the greatest servants are leaders. All of the greatest leaders are servants.

CHAPTER NINETEEN

Faith or Logic

Is God reasonable?

Now faith is being sure of what we hope for and certain of what we do not see. Hebrews 11:1

To be called a logical person is a compliment. It means you are reasonable, able to see the natural progression of a presentation, and draw the proper conclusion. Logical people understand syllogisms. A syllogism is an argument based on two related and factual statements which, when combined, form a natural conclusion. Before you scream and flip to the next chapter, consider this simple example: All trees have roots. An oak is a type of tree. Therefore an oak tree has roots. See, you are more logical that you thought!

Now let's try syllogistic thinking on a more important theme.

1. All people sin.
2. Those who sin go to hell.
3. All people are going to hell.

Wow! I don't like the way that one turned out. Let's try another syllogism with a more positive premise.

1. All people do some good things and some bad things.
2. Good people go to heaven.
3. Those who do more good things than bad things go to heaven.

That one I can live with. It makes sense. No one can do all good and no wrong. If there are people in heaven, it stands to reason they must have done more good than bad. Those who have done more bad things than good things must be the ones who go to hell ... assuming, of course, there is such a place as hell. It all makes perfect sense, but salvation by personal effort is contrary to everything the Bible teaches.

The Bible says, "There is a way that seems right to a man, but in the end it leads to death." God considered that message so important it is repeated word for word in two different verses: Proverbs 14:12 and 16:25. In other words, when it comes to the ways of God, faith—not logic—is the driving force. Logic says we are saved by doing good. Faith says we are not.

If doing more good than bad is *not* the key to salvation, then how are sinners saved? Salvation requires perfection. That's right, *perfection*. Jesus said, "Be perfect, therefore, as your heavenly Father is perfect" (Matthew 5:48). But the Bible also says, "If we claim to be without sin, we deceive ourselves and the truth is not in us" (1 John 1:8). How can God expect us to be something that He says is impossible? The syllogism is not hopeful.

1. You must be perfect to get to heaven.
2. No one is perfect.
3. No one is going to heaven.

That syllogism *makes sense* and *is biblical.* How can anyone be saved? The logical answer is not hard to understand: Without the help of a Savior no one can be saved. Paul called it a "gift" which comes by grace (undeserved love) through faith (confident hope) in Jesus whom the Bible says took our sin upon Himself and gave us His perfection. (Cf. Ephesians 2:8–10 and 2 Corinthians 5:21.)

Paul explained it this way: "Whatever was to my profit [the good stuff in his favor] I now consider loss for the sake of Christ. What is more, I consider everything a loss compared to the surpassing greatness of knowing Christ Jesus my Lord, for whose sake I have lost all things. I consider them rubbish, that I may gain Christ and be found in Him, *not having a righteousness of my own that comes from the law, but that which is through faith in Christ*—the righteousness that comes from God and is by faith" (Philippians 3:7–9, emphasis added).

God turns everything around. Instead of doing good things to get to heaven, He gives us heaven so we can do good things—"Without faith it is impossible to please God" (Hebrews 11:6). He didn't save us because of who we are or what we've done but because of who He is and what He's done. The good things Christians do are not done to acquire a gift they already possess. They do good things out of gratitude for the perfection God has already given them by grace through faith in Jesus. Christians still make mistakes. Christians still sin, but their sins won't keep them out of heaven. Perfection is a gift received by grace through faith in Jesus, not something achieved. The syllogism goes like this.

1. All perfect people go to heaven.
2. Those who believe in Jesus are perfectly forgiven.
3. All who believe in Jesus go to heaven.

No wonder those who believe in Jesus will endure everything—even death—rather than deny their faith. Paul said, "The life I live in the body, I live by faith in the Son of God, who loved me and gave Himself for me" (Galatians 2:20). He told the Christians at Corinth, "Christ's love compels us" (2 Corinthians 5:14). It compelled Paul through some pretty difficult situations, even death by martyrdom.

The love of Christ also compelled Paul Gerhardt. Against all logic, tragedy deepened—never weakened—his faith in God. You may not know Gerhardt's name but you probably know a hymn or two he wrote. More of Gerhardt's hymns have been translated into English than any other German composer, even Martin Luther.

Gerhardt wrote incredible hymns. Twenty-one of them were included in the hymnal of my childhood. Maybe you've sung a few of them yourself:

"I Will Sing My Maker's Praises"
"O Lord, How Shall I Meet Thee"
"All My Heart This Night Rejoices"
"O Jesus Christ, Thy Manger Is"
"Come, Your Hearts and Voices Raising"
"We Sing, Immanuel, Thy Praise"
"Now Let Us Come before Him"
"A Lamb Goes Uncomplaining Forth"
"Upon the Cross Extended"
"O Sacred Head, Now Wounded"
"Awake, My Heart, with Gladness"
"Oh, Enter Lord, Thy Temple"
"Jesus, Thy Boundless Love"
"Commit Whatever Grieves Thee"
"Why Should Cross and Trial Grieve Me?"
"If God Himself Be for Me"
"Rejoice My Heart Be Glad and Sing"
"Now Rest Beneath Night's Shadows"
"O Lord, I Sing with Lips and Heart"
"All Ye Who on This Earth Do Dwell"
"A Pilgrim and a Stranger"

Paul Gerhardt was born on March 12, 1607, in a small village near Wittenberg. Today a life-sized portrait of Gerhardt hangs in the Lutheran church at Luebden where he died on June 7, 1676. Beneath the portrait are inscribed the words, "Theologus in cribro Satanae versatus." The Latin phrase means, "A theologian sifted by Satan's sieve." You might think that's a strange epitaph. But then again, if you knew more about the life of Paul Gerhardt, you might not.

Gerhardt's father, Christian Gerhardt, was mayor of their little village, but he died when Paul was very young. Paul was raised by his mother and her family during one of the darkest periods of European history. The Thirty Years War ravaged Europe from 1618 until 1648. Fighting largely over religious differences, the Protestants, Lutherans, and Roman Catholic princes battled to gain land and maintain control of the faith in regions over which they reigned.

Nearly half of all European citizens died either in the fighting or because of starvation brought about by devastation of the land. The suffering was extreme. Five of Paul Gerhardt's six children preceded him in death, four of them dying in infancy. His wife, Anna Marie, was so devastated by the emotional toll, she succumbed, dying shortly after the death of their fourth child.

As if personal struggle was not enough, Gerhardt was subject to the constant attack and discouragement of a jealous colleague. Gerhardt was considered the most popular Lutheran preacher in Berlin, but his elector (a Calvinist) required all pastors to swear an oath and sign a document pledging they would not preach on doctrinal differences between the two beliefs. Gerhardt, advanced in age and ill, would not sign the document and urged his colleagues to stand their ground. Despite Gerhardt's popularity and the elector's respect for the hymn writer and theologian, the elector's hands were tied by the edict. Gerhardt was removed from his pulpit and forced to resign his pastorate.

Instead of enjoying the respect his speaking, writing, and faithfulness merited, the elderly Gerhardt was forced to begin over in another province. He took the position at Luebden and served a congregation described as a rough and unsympa-

thizing people. It was there he died eight years later. Did the
years of hardship harden the man? No. The hardship deepened the pastor/poet's love for his Savior. The year that his
fourth child died, Gerhardt wrote his famous Christmas hymn,

"Come, your hearts and voices raising,
Christ the Lord with gladness praising;
Loudly sing His love amazing,
Worthy folk of Christendom.

Sin and death may well be groaning,
Satan now may well be moaning;
We, our full salvation owning,
Cast our ev'ry care away."[49]

In the Old Testament a man named Job lost his wealth and
his family but continued to pray. His wife logically challenged
his sanity, saying, "Are you still holding on to your integrity?
Curse God and die!" (Job 2:9) Job, shaken but not without
hope, responded, "You are talking like a foolish woman. Shall
we accept good from God, and not trouble? ... Though He slay
me, yet will I hope in Him" (Job 2:10, 13:15). Logic isn't
always the answer, and faith isn't always logical.

When the disciples of Jesus came upon a man who was
blind from the day of his birth, they asked a logical question,
"Rabbi, who sinned, this man or his parents, that he was born
blind?" (John 9:2) It made sense. If something so tragic happened, there must be a reason. Somebody, somewhere must
have done something wrong. Jesus answered them, "Neither
this man nor his parents sinned, ... but this happened so that
the work of God might be displayed in his life" (John 9:3).
Jesus then healed the man who became (as foretold by Jesus)
a powerful and sincere witness to the deity of Christ.

According to his book, *When Bad Things Happen to Good*

People, Rabbi Kushner would have a hard time accepting Jesus' explanation for the blind man's handicap and Jesus' miracle which granted him sight. The rabbi logically concludes trouble comes in order to bring people together, or to bring out a person's inner hidden strength. Fate, he says, not God is in control of things and there are some things God can't or won't do.[50] Even religious people sometimes wrongly count on logic to explain the illogical, and reason to explain matters of faith.

Logically, Paul Gerhardt might have concluded there was no value in faith so why believe? But the persecuted pastor wasn't interested in understanding all the whys or wherefores of his life. He knew "God is love" (1 John 4:8). He also knew God didn't cause all things but, "In all things God works for the good of those who love Him, who have been called according to His purpose" (Romans 8:28). He didn't believe because faith helped him understand life. He maintained his faith because life didn't make sense. He could say with Paul, "I consider that our present sufferings are not worth comparing with the glory that will be revealed in us" (Romans 8:18).

As Solomon said, "There is a way that seems right to a man, but in the end it leads to death" (Proverbs 14:12). Doing more good things than bad things may seem to be the logical answer to life and the key to life eternal. But logic isn't always God's way. God's ways are quite often contrary to popular belief. After all, faith according to God's definition is "being sure of what we hope for and certain of *what we do not see*" (Hebrews 11:1, emphasis added). Faith, not logic saves.

CHAPTER TWENTY

Winners or Losers

When you lose, you win!

Blessed are you when people insult you, persecute you and falsely say all kinds of evil against you because of Me. Rejoice and be glad, because great is your reward in heaven, for in the same way they persecuted the prophets who were before you. Matthew 5:11–12

Sometimes when you win you lose, and when you lose you win. Jesus told His disciples, "Whoever wants to save his life will lose it, but whoever loses his life for Me and for the Gospel will save it" (Mark 8:35). Here's how the Living Bible paraphrased that sometimes confusing verse: "If you insist on saving your life, you will lose it. Only those who throw away their lives for My sake and for the sake of the Good News will ever know what it means to really live."

Can you really win by losing and lose by winning? It all depends on what you are trying to win. I doubt there was ever anyone who knew more about winning than Knute Kenneth Rockne, head football coach of Notre Dame. Many believe he may have been the best motivator of young men ever to coach a college football team. Before his tragic death in a plane crash, Coach Rockne posted incredible numbers. As head coach of the Notre Dame football team for thirteen years he won 105 games, lost only twelve, and tied in five. His team won three national championships and went undefeated in five of his thirteen seasons. Although he knew a great deal about winning, Rockne didn't pretend to know much at all about losing. Once, when pressed by reporters to explain a rare loss, the coach said he wouldn't know why they'd lost until after he talked to his barber on Monday.

Rockne's name will be forever associated with another great winner, George Gipp, team captain of the 1919 and 1920 Fighting Irish football team. Rockne first noticed Gipp punting a ball to another student in an open field. Rockne was then assistant football coach to Jesse Harper, and he urged Gipp to try out for the team. The rest is history.

When Rockne took over head coaching responsibilities in 1919, he learned his captain-elect had been suspended for missing too many classes. Gipp complained that he had been ill and if given the chance he could prove he knew the material. Rockne got him the chance and good to his word, Gipp passed with flying colors. The team went undefeated as its coach and star player rallied them. In 1920, things only got better. Undefeated again, Gipp led his school in a romp over their tough rival Army with a personal best of 357 yards.

The effort, the practice, and the severe conditions of outdoor play did what no opponent could—sideline George Gipp. Just weeks before the end of his senior season, Gipp was hospitalized for a severe throat infection. Feeling better before the game, Gipp suited up and joined the team on the sidelines. Neither Rockne nor Gipp expected the star to play. The fans could not be quieted, however, so the coach relented and let Gipp run a few plays. The infection returned with a vengeance, and without the aid of modern antibiotics, it quickly developed into pneumonia. Three weeks later, on December 14, 1920, George Gipp died.

Before he died, Gipp absolved his beloved coach of any responsibility. In some of his last words he told his friend and mentor, "Rock, some day when things look real tough for Notre Dame, ask the boys to go out there and win one for the Gipper." His words are remembered and quoted by people who have long forgotten the story behind them.

Have you ever wanted something or someone so much that you were willing to die for it if necessary? Jesus described that as the greatest kind of love. It was the kind of love He had for us. George Gipp died for a man and a team he loved. He didn't intend to, but it happened. More incredible than that, Jesus willingly died for those who despised Him. Paul described Jesus' sacrifice by saying, "Very rarely will anyone die for a righteous man, though for a good man someone might possibly dare to die. But God demonstrates His own love for us in this: While we were still sinners, Christ died for us" (Romans 5:7–8).

Understanding the nature of Jesus' sacrifice helped Paul through his own difficult days. Even before his martyrdom, Paul walked away from a lucrative and potentially powerful position. Though only a young man, he was rising to the top of his profession faster than any of his peers. Like a young promising lawyer today, there seemed no end to his potential. Then he met the Lord.

While Paul carried out his duty for those he was trying so hard to impress, the Lord literally knocked him to the ground, took away his sight, his misguided zeal, and his future. In just one afternoon Paul went from top of the heap to bottom of the barrel. What could possibly be worth such sacrifice? Paul described his feelings about that day to the Christians at Philippi, "Whatever was to my profit I now consider loss for the sake of Christ. What is more, I consider everything a loss compared to the surpassing greatness of knowing Christ Jesus my Lord, for whose sake I have lost all things. I consider them rubbish, that I may gain Christ and be found in Him, not having a righteousness of my own that comes from the law, but that which is through faith in Christ—the righteousness that comes from God and is by faith" (Philippians 3:7–9).

For Paul, losing status among his peers was nothing compared to all he gained through faith in Christ. The things he had once considered so important seemed like rubbish. In Paul's life losing was winning.

Is the sacrifice worth the benefit? It depends on what you are trying to achieve. For Paul, the greatest of all moments would be the upward call of Jesus on the day of his death. Did he ever regret the cost? Not at all. He told the Christians at Rome, "I consider that our present sufferings are not worth comparing with the glory that will be revealed in us" (Romans 8:18).

Paul's gain may look like loss to those outside of saving faith. Good things are often mistaken for loss by those on the outside looking in.

When I married Carol I gave up hanging out with my buddies. I no longer went on midnight runs for burgers or stayed up all night shooting billiards in the basement of the college dorm. True, my once stellar Ping-Pong game fell a notch, and my standing on the intramural squads and church leagues became less important. To some, I suppose, giving up those things would be chalked up as a loss, but to those who know the love and support of a faithful spouse, it is clearly a win.

When Joshua and Jacob were born into our family they brought along a world of change. We gave up uninterrupted sleep and the spontaneity of last-minute dates. Mealtime took on a life of its own, and laundry duty came faster than snowflakes in a blizzard. For a good number of years I gave up regular participation in hobbies such as golf, hunting, and fishing in exchange for Little League, soccer, and Frisbee. Carol gave up freedom-of-schedule to taxi kids here and chaperone kids there. These days she gives up transportation altogether so the boys can take her car on their social outings. To some, I suppose, giving up those things would be chalked up as a loss, but to those who know the love and joy of children, it is clearly a win.

When the demands of seminary study and congregational ministry came along, I gave up my need to know the exact standings of my favorite teams. Though I was an athlete and sports enthusiast, it became easier and easier to miss an important game without feeling any sense of sacrifice. Today I still enjoy the opportunity to watch a game or visit the stadium, but I'd just as soon see a movie, visit a friend, or work in the garden with Carol. To some, I suppose, giving up those things would be chalked up as a loss, but to those who know the satisfaction and rewards of ministry, it is clearly a win.

I am not suggesting that Christians are good losers, neither was Knute Rockne. He once said, "Show me a gracious loser and I'll show you a failure." The Christian faith is not about losing. The old hymn says, "The strife is o'er, the battle done; Now is the victor's triumph won; Now be the song of praise begun. Alleluia!"[51]

When John was granted his revelation on the isle of Patmos he encountered an incredible vision of the victorious Jesus in all His glory. Jesus spoke to John saying, "Do not be afraid. I am the First and the Last. I am the Living One; I was dead, and behold I am alive for ever and ever! And I hold the keys of death and Hades" (Revelation 1:17–18). The Christian faith is not about losing, just the opposite. As proof of His victory Jesus displayed the keys of death and hell.

Those in the Lord's camp are the victors. It is easy to identify the winners. They're the ones holding the prize. There is no greater prize than the reward of eternal joy. Nothing on earth compares. "What good is it," Jesus asked, "For a man to gain the whole world, yet forfeit his soul? Or what can a man give in exchange for his soul? If anyone is ashamed of Me and My words in this adulterous and sinful generation, the Son of Man will be ashamed of him when He comes in His Father's glory with the holy angels" (Mark 8:36–38).

Can you really win by losing and lose by winning? It all depends on what you are trying to win.

CHAPTER TWENTY-ONE

Punishment or Discipline

Sometimes love hurts.

Endure hardship as discipline; God is treating you as sons. For what son is not disciplined by his father? Hebrews 12:7

I always enjoy talking with people who work with the public. They are storehouses of information about human nature. Howard qualifies on several counts. He grew up working for his daddy who managed public golf courses. Today he's a respected professional photographer, and when time allows, he helps a local law enforcement agency patrol his Texas community. Howard has learned a lot about people by observation.

In his own amusing way Howard told me the story of a woman who had lost all control of her children. "Stephen," he said, "I know that Jesus loves her and He died on the cross for her the same as me. I know that we are brothers and sisters in Christ, and I'm not supposed to judge and all that—but the woman is a complete idiot! She's a very wealthy lady, and everywhere she goes she takes a nanny along so that if the kids need correcting someone is there to do it. She told me that she doesn't want to discipline them herself because it might hurt their relationship. Once she wanted a special picture taken of her children in Victorian-style clothes. Her daughter looked just fine, but the young boy showed up in blue jeans and his favorite pair of Nike shoes because she couldn't make him change his clothes. Sometimes," Howard observed, "people can be downright peculiar."

Howard was seeing firsthand the early stages of what psychologists call Spoiled Child Syndrome. The *Journal of the American Academy of Pediatrics* has coined the term to describe those children who are "excessively self-centered and immature." The parents of such children have lost control. The inmates are running the asylum.

The mother of an incorrigible four-year-old described how her daughter had taken over the house. The girl had been dismissed from two preschools for uncontrollable behavior, so the mother quit work to stay home with her. Now if mom asks her daughter to do anything distasteful, the hellion jumps up and down on her bed and tells her mother to get out of *her* house. She tells *her mother* when she's ready for bed, what *she* wants to eat, and exactly what *she* wants her mom to purchase *for her*. Mom doesn't know what to do anymore. How did things get so wrong? Psychologists have identified at least five root causes for role reversal between parents and their children.

In almost every home where role reversal occurs, both parents are working. This is not a problem for the majority of people, but for a few it creates a guilt complex that can lead to role reversal. Absent parents will lose control of children they rarely see. A research organization, making a study of juvenile delinquency, telephoned fifty homes between 9:30 and 10:30 p.m. to ask parents if they knew where their children were. Half of the calls were answered by children who had no idea where their parents were.

Imitation, the most basic form of learning, has been denied

many parents who grew up in small families and never observed their parents raising younger brothers and sisters.

Corporate transfers and career opportunities that keep the family moving upset the stability of the home. The frequent moves often produce guilt in parents and a more permissive attitude toward children who complain about how unfair and insensitive mom and dad have been.

Some parents turn their children into demigods by paying too much attention to their wants and desires. All family activity revolves around the child's sport, hobbies, and school activities, causing imbalance and a belief by the child (especially in small families) that the world revolves around his or her schedule.

Materialism is out of control. In 1800, seventy-five percent of all family income was spent on food. By 1850 it had fallen to fifty percent, and today's basic provision requires only ten percent of the average American's income. Add the availability of credit and you have a society that can buy whatever it wants with cash, credit, or on the monthly installment plan.

Discipline is not a bad word. The evening news continually reports horrifying stories of crack-addicted mothers neglecting their children or violent accounts of stepfathers or live-in boyfriends who have sexually abused, beaten, or shaken a child to death. In repulsion, many parents have sworn never to discipline their children and have become overly permissive.

The St. Louis Division of Family Services understands that both extremes can be harmful for the child. Personnel who answer their child-abuse hotline are trained to respond to children trying to blackmail their parents. From time to time an out-of-control child will call, or a parent will call and explain that his or her child has been threatening to call and then put the child on the line. Although they take every call seriously and watch for repeat disturbances, the hotline staff is not anti-discipline. They affirm that mild spanking is not against the law. (Missouri State Law specifically allows "spanking administered in a reasonable manner.")[52] Second, they commend parents for having their children call and want them to know they are trained to recognize blackmail when they hear it. Third, they support a parent's right to establish rules and expect their children to live within the rules so long as abuse does not occur.

Too many people use the terms punishment and discipline interchangeably. Punishment is not the same as discipline. Punishment implies retribution. When a child is punished he is made to "pay a price" for his disobedience by means of pain or emotional trauma. Discipline focuses on the child, not the wrong. Corrective measures are taken not because a child "deserves it," but because the behavior or the child is detrimental to others and the child herself. The word discipline comes from the same Latin word for disciple and literally means "to teach or guide."

God does not punish Christians for their sins. Jesus endured our punishment when God "canceled the written code, with its regulations, that was against us and that stood opposed to us; He took it away, nailing it to the cross" (Colossians 2:14). God does not *punish* Christians but He *disciplines* those He loves. The Bible compares divine discipline to the love parents show their children through discipline in healthy homes.

> "Those whom the Lord loves He disciplines, and He scourges[53] every son whom He receives." It is for discipline that you endure; God deals with you as with sons; for what son is there whom his father does not discipline? But if you are without discipline, of which all have become partakers, then you are illegitimate children and

not sons. Furthermore, we had earthly fathers to discipline us, and we respected them; shall we not much rather be subject to the Father of spirits, and live? For they disciplined us for a short time as seemed best to them, but He disciplines us for our good, that we may share His holiness. All discipline for the moment seems not to be joyful, but sorrowful; yet to those who have been trained by it, afterwards it yields the peaceful fruit of righteousness. (Hebrews 12:6–11, NASB)

The Bible makes some interesting observations. First, God loves us like a parent loves his child. Second, parents communicate love to their children through discipline as well as affirmation. Third, those children who grow up without discipline will feel unloved and rejected. Fourth, we learn to respect our parents and our Lord through the discipline we receive. And last, discipline, when experienced, seems wrong but in the end we are better off because of it.

A parent who observes her child with other children throwing rocks at the neighbor's dog will respond in predictable fashion. She will stop the behavior, send the other children packing, and discipline her child. She may require her son or daughter to write a note of apology and walk with her next door to deliver it in person along with a verbal explanation. She may even ask her child to take some of his allowance and buy the neighbor's dog a treat, making amends for his mistake. Why would a parent expect more from her child than the other children who were just as guilty? She expects more of her child because she loves him and cares about the attitudes and behaviors he will value the rest of his life. As the passage says, the parent who doesn't discipline a child is communicating lack of concern, but parental love cares too much to let a child continue a self-destructive activity.

Children need discipline as much as they need hugs. Those raised without discipline will instinctively misbehave until discipline is applied. We call it "crying out for attention" or "acting out." Parents wise enough to discipline a child for minor offenses often save themselves and their children the consequence of more serious offenses.

God deals with us as His children. If you've ever thought that God seems to frustrate and correct your behavior more often than He bothers those who don't care a thing about Jesus, you may be right. True, "[God] wants all men to be saved and to come to a knowledge of the truth" (1 Timothy 2:4). But like that parent who sent the other children away while she disciplined her own, so God takes a special interest in His children. He protects us from self-destructive behaviors and self-centered values that are dangerous to our faith. He stirs our conscience and frustrates our path. David experienced this special kind of divine love and described it by saying, "Blessed is the man whose sin the LORD does not count against him and in whose spirit is no deceit. When I kept silent, my bones wasted away through my groaning all day long. For day and night Your hand was heavy upon me; my strength was sapped as in the heat of summer. Then I acknowledged my sin to You and did not cover up my iniquity. I said, 'I will confess my transgressions to the LORD'—and You forgave the guilt of my sin" (Psalm 32:2–5). Before David repented he felt the hand of God opposing him day and night. If Hallmark "Cares Enough to Send the Very Best," by contrast the Lord sometimes "Cares Enough to Send the Worst." Not every Christian hardship is a result of God's discipline, but like David we should let hardship serve as a catalyst for reflection and prayer.

It is important to remember that discipline is not punishment. Isaiah tells us, "He [the Messiah, Jesus] was pierced for our transgressions, He was crushed for our iniquities; the punishment that brought us peace was upon Him, and by His wounds we are healed. We all, like sheep, have gone astray, each of us has turned to His own way; and the LORD has laid on Him the iniquity of us all" (Isaiah 53:5–6). God is not sadistic. He does not extract second payment for sins already covered by the death of Jesus. Paul used this truth to emphasize the grace of God in His letter to the Christians at Galatia. "I do not set aside the grace of God, for if righteousness could be gained through the law, Christ died for nothing!" (Galatians 2:21) In other words, if Christ died for me, then the price is already paid and I will not be judged on the basis of my good works or my faults.

As you discipline your children, make sure your motive is for their betterment, not to extract payment for your anger or embarrassment. Make sure your motive is the same as God's, who disciplines us so that we won't stray from His holiness. As our sons can attest, Carol and I have always believed in the value of discipline exercised in love. Some of our guiding principles have included:

1. Never discipline when you're angry. Although immediate intervention may be required it is sometimes best to wait before assigning discipline.
2. Always talk through the situation and explain your expectation for proper behavior.
3. Give your children the opportunity to chose between behavior and discipline. "You can clean your room or leave it dirty and miss the party. The decision is up to you."
4. Never use public embarrassment as a form of discipline.
5. Never let children behave differently (rudely) in public. If they want to embarrass themselves it is perfectly fine and you should not disappoint them.
6. Never hit in anger. A swat on the bottom is not abuse

but as children become more verbal, your discipline should become more articulate.

7. Keep your voice calm. It helps children stay calm and keeps the discussion focused.
8. Listen to their side of the story. You need to know how they think and why they believed their inappropriate behavior was okay.
9. Explain to teenagers that you are answerable to God for your parenting. When they are parents they can be more permissive or do it differently.
10. Give hugs, affirm your love, and accentuate the positive after the discipline has had its effect. Remember discipline is not the same as punishment which makes a person pay or suffer in proportion to their wrong.

Love and discipline go hand in hand. You really can't have one without the other. That's a position that's contrary to popular belief. As the Bible says, "No discipline seems pleasant at the time, but painful." We are inclined to ask, "How could someone who loves me make my life difficult?" But the passage continues, "Later on, however, it [discipline] produces a harvest of righteousness and peace for those who have been trained by it" (Hebrews 12:11).

When we care about people, we care about what becomes of them. Because we care about what becomes of our children we are willing to practice discipline. Can we, as God's children, expect any less from our heavenly Father? "Our [earthly] fathers disciplined us for a little while as they thought best; but God disciplines us for our good, that we may share in His holiness" (Hebrews 12:10). Thank God for discipline.

CHAPTER TWENTY-TWO

Creation or Evolution

Why can't someone decide?

By faith we understand that the universe was formed at God's command, so that what is seen was not made out of what was visible. Hebrews 11:3

It could happen on just about any high school or university campus. A professor, concluding a series on the origins of life and the work of Charles Darwin, takes time to review the pertinent facts.

Standing at the front of the class, chalk in hand, he walks to the board and begins, "So let's review the basic tenets of the evolutionary theory." As he talks, he writes five suppositions on the board for the benefit of his class.

First—"The Big Bang Theory":

Scientists concur that the universe is continuing its course towards rapid expansion. Astronomers have shown the galaxies nearest the earth are moving away from each other at an enormous rate. By tracking backward movement we calculate the original explosion creating the universe occurred 20 billion years ago.

Second—Simple life evolved into more complex species:

Single-celled life-forms evolved to multicelled life-forms. Water-borne life became amphibious, then land-dwelling, and eventually even flight-capable.

Third—Survival of the fittest and natural selection are the basis for the evolutionary theory:

The process of natural selection describes the means by which the smarter, the stronger, and the faster survived as the weaker and inferior became extinct.

Fourth—The glacial age, or ice age, brought a sudden end to the era commonly known as prehistoric.

Paleontology is the study of the fossil record which verifies the evolutionary process. The fossil record supports the ice-age theory, indicating a sudden end to certain life-forms both plant and animal. All geological evidence confirms this to be true.

Fifth—Man, the most advanced of all species, has evolved over millions of years from primates:

The fossil record is replete with transitional life-forms verifying this link with our prehistoric past.

Concluding his comments, he turns toward the class. "Any questions or comments, please?"

After a brief pause the professor notices some murmuring in the back corner of the room. A number of the students appear to be urging a classmate to comment. The professor turns and walks toward the distraction. "Well, Miss Jones, do you have something to say, or is it a private conversation between friends?" The rest of the class chuckles at their fellow student's embarrassment.

"We were just talking ..." answers Miss Jones. "We were talking about this class in the university commons last night, and we aren't sure we can believe all this business about billions of years and the tired evolutionary theory of natural selection and survival of the fittest."

"Oh no," groans the professor. "You went to Biiiiible study, did you? How long have you been a university student anyway? Don't tell me you believe in some God who created heaven and earth in six days!" His mocking tone is not lost on the class as he feigns surprise at her simplistic thinking. "This is not your mama's church, Miss Jones. This is a class established for scientific study. Here we study empirical evidence, concrete, factual, provable data. If you want religion, you're in the wrong class."

The room grows silent. The students turn in their chairs to watch the confrontation as their professor stops his little tirade next to the questioning student's desk. Not completely intimidated, Miss Jones opens her spiral notebook and continues.

"I am a Christian," she begins, "and I agree with you about the purpose of this class. We should stick to a discussion of scientific facts and those things that can be proven."

"Very good," the professor replies. "What's your question?"

"Well," glancing at her nearby friends for support, Miss Jones continues, "we wrote down some questions that we wanted to ask." The rest of her friends join in the discussion.

A nearby friend asks, "If the earth began with an explosion of gasses, where did the gasses come from and what caused them to explode?"

"No one knows for sure," the professor answers calmly.

"If simple life-forms evolved into more complex life, why

aren't there transitional life-forms evident in our world today? Shouldn't we have half-monkey, half-people life-forms still evolving? Why are species becoming extinct instead of more plentiful?"

Growing uneasy, the professor moves back to the safety of his desk and away from the dissension. "Some scientists speculate that evolution happens in spurts and only under ideal conditions. It may even discontinue for a time. No one is sure," he answers.

"Have scientists ever been able to create organic life from inorganic materials?" asks another.

"They have been able to reorganize various virus forms and cause them to flourish in living cells," the professor responds. "But, to be honest, no one has been able to combine chemicals or inorganic elements in such a way to create a new life-form. An argument from silence, however, is no proof that it didn't happen," he quickly adds.

"An argument from silence is no proof that it did happen either," comments a student sitting near the front of the room. The rebellion seems to be growing.

"Doesn't the Second Law of Thermodynamics hold that every energy transformation results in less energy being available, which means that ultimately there will be no energy available at all? Applied to the theory of evolution it would mean things move from complex to simple, not from simple to complex. And isn't it true that mutations lead to a deterioration not an improvement of the species and mutant life-forms are less fit, not more fit for survival?" The students have obviously done some research on their questions, and the professor senses an organized effort to discredit his lecture series.

"You are confusing two very different scientific theories," he answers. "The laws of thermodynamics have no relevant application in evolutionary theory. We are talking about millions of years. You must understand that different natural laws may have been present in the prehistoric past which are not observable today. Differing environmental conditions may also explain long suspensions of the evolutionary process. Now let's get back to our notes."

"Professor." Another student has a question. "Those transitional life-forms we've been studying have all been proven to be fraudulent. Java Man was created from a thigh bone, a skull, and a tooth. Even when it was presented in 1894, ten scientists said it was an ape, seven said it was a man, and only seven others said it was a missing link. Before his death its discoverer Eugene Dubois said it was only the skeletal remains of a giant gibbon," the student reads from his notes. "Piltdown man was also proved to be a fake. Oxford professors proved it was a human skull joined to a chimpanzee's jaw with its teeth filed down and the whole thing stained with iron salts. Nebraska man, the great proof of Clarence Darrow in the Scopes Trial, was a total fabrication from a single tooth which was later proven to be from a wild pig."

"We still have Lucy!" The professor interrupts a bit defensively.

"But Lucy is nothing more than an artist's rendering of a prehistoric woman based on bones that were found from different sites several miles apart and at different earth levels! How can anyone claim they came from even the same species, let alone the exact same person or animal?"

"Paleontology is not a perfect science, young man." The professor's irritation is now clearly visible. "It is an ongoing process of discovery and evaluation. To be sure, evolution is a theory that is itself evolving over time. But evolution and its theories remain the very best explanation of life's origin, based on man's rational attempt to understand his prehistoric past. There is no room in science for any wild notions of miracles and spirits 'moving over the face of the deep.' This is a science class, and it will remain a science class. Do I make myself clear? End of discussion!"

Students in need of grades from professors in positions of authority are not likely to engage in such a dynamic debate, but they could. Despite what many believe, the Bible is not without explanation to the origins of life. Its primary purpose is to explain and accomplish the salvation of the world by grace through faith in the Messiah, Jesus. Yet even the teaching of salvation has its roots in the story of creation and the sin of Adam and Eve. The Genesis record tells us, "God saw all that He had made, and it was very good" (Genesis 1:31). Adam and Eve were perfect (without sin) and placed in a perfect world which God had created for their existence. The establishment of the world by means of divine creation is not a minor "optional" teaching of the Bible. Creation by the hand of God is used in the New Testament to define faith. The Bible says, "Now faith is being sure of what we hope for and certain of what we do not see. This is what the ancients were commended for. By faith we understand that the universe was formed at God's command, so that what is seen was not made out of what was visible" (Hebrews 11:1–3).

Christians and nonbelievers will by definition approach this subject from different perspectives, but that is not the same as saying Christians reject good science. Good science, like good history, good archaeology, and good paleontology, will confirm—not contradict—the truth of Scripture. There are some who argue that evolution, not theology, is most threatened by the scientific method of "problem-hypothesis-test."

Paul Zimmerman, former president of my alma mater, wrote an essay on the subject of creation in which he referenced a study of the French scientist Lecomte du Nouy.

> A decade ago the French scientist Lecomte du Nouy examined the mathematical odds of life having evolved by chance from nonliving material. His calculations involved the probability of the formation of a single protein molecule by chance. Du Nouy concluded that the odds against the formation of a single protein molecule were so large as to be virtually equivalent to the utterly impossible. He reported that the, "time needed to form, on an average, one such molecule in material volume equal to that of our terrestrial globe is 10[BB2]^{243} *billions* of years." (This is equivalent to one billion followed by 243 zeroes.) In other words a period of time would be required that is fantastically longer than even 2.5 billion years currently estimated as the time at which life began. Moreover, these figures are for *one* protein molecule. A single cell needs millions of them and other complex molecules! Du Nouy states, "If the probability of appearance of a living *cell* could be expressed mathematically, the preceding figures would seem negligible."[54]

Darwin was not a scientist. His only earned degree was in the field of theology for which he studied at Cambridge from 1828 to 1831. Upon graduation he accompanied a British ship on a scientific exploration of the world for five years. The observations he made as the ship's naturalist served as the basis for conclusions he would draw in his watershed work, *The Origin of Species,* published in 1859. His work proved to be more philosophical than scientific. He provided no support for his theory, included no scientific evidence, and cited no samples of transitional life-forms. It was, however, a theory the world seemed waiting to embrace. The first printing of Darwin's book sold out on the very first day.

There were skeptics, including Darwin himself. In his book *Evolution Is Not Scientific,* Albert Sippert quotes Darwin as saying, "There are 2 or 3 million species on earth, sufficient field, one might think, for observation. But it must be said today that in spite of all the efforts of trained observers not one change of a species into another is on record."[55] Sippert was also unimpressed by the language of assumption and speculation used by Darwin in *The Origin of Species,* especially chapter four. Phrases common to Darwin's hypotheses include, "If... If assumed... It seems, therefore extremely probably... If we suppose... may have been... perhaps... probably... we may suppose... it is probable... etc." Sippert concludes his assessment of Darwin's research with the understatement, "This is not the way a scientist speaks. A scientist works on the basis of tested, proven facts."[56]

I once read in a science textbook that if everyone in the world joined together to count the atoms in a single drop of water, with all five billion people counting one atom apiece every second, the task would take more than 30,000 years to complete. Is such a microscopic and miraculous world the result of divine creation or random evolution? Either way it comes down to faith.

Will you believe that spontaneously generated matter somehow exploded in a "big bang," resulting in conditions as complex as our universe? Could such a theory adequately explain the complex and microscopic elements necessary for life, including the double helix of DNA that governs how protein synthesis will uniquely occur in billions of living cells? Is such a theory truly reasonable? Or will you put your faith in the time-tested and proven Scriptures which simply state, "In the beginning God created the heaven and the earth" (Genesis 1:1).

Sometimes what's right seems wrong. But sometimes, upon closer examination, what's right makes the best sense of all.

CHAPTER TWENTY-THREE

Foolish or Wise

Christians do the dumbest things.

*The fear of the LORD is the beginning of wisdom;
all who follow His precepts have good understanding. To Him belongs eternal praise. Psalm
111:10*

It happened in Italy in the late 1940s. The very successful and well-known author Dr. A.J. Cronin was enjoying vaca-
tion with friends.

They visited Tivoli, the ancient retreat of Roman emperors,
with its huge renaissance gardens, its great cathedral, and the
temple of Vesta. Cronin toured Hadrian's Villa and enjoyed the
excitement of the cafes on the Via Veneto. Concerning the
famous avenue he wrote, "[It] throbbed with color and excitement—sleek cars in slow procession, cafés filled with a fash-
ionable throng, flower stalls riotous with blossoms."[57] He saw
it all and did it all.

The most important site the famous author visited while
vacationing in Italy came by accident. The day it happened
Cronin had spent the early afternoon enjoying a luncheon
with other friends at their villa several miles from Rome. As
he returned to Rome, Cronin became lost and decided to stop
and ask for direction. It wasn't long before he noticed a rather
small, square, gray stone building set apart from the rest.
Assuming it to be a small government building of some kind,
he stopped and entered. It didn't take long to realize he had
entered a different kind of public place, a small but ancient

Christian church. He had been to the great cathedral of St. Peter and the great basilicas of St. Paul and St. Clement. Despite its plain appearance the small narthex had an air of sacredness that kept Cronin from quickly leaving.

As his eyes adjusted to the dimly lit room, Cronin noticed a bronze plaque embedded in the well-worn stone floor. Although almost obliterated from wear, he could make out the Latin words, "Quo Vadis." Suddenly he realized the importance of his chance visit.

According to legend it was on this very spot that the apostle Peter, fleeing Rome and the persecution of Nero, had encountered a vision of the resurrected Christ. Stunned by the apparition, Peter reportedly asked in his typical, awkward way, "Quo Vadis, Lord?"—"Whither goest Thou, Lord?" According to tradition, the Lord told Peter He was traveling to Rome to encourage the faithful who were being martyred by Nero. The Lord, turning to Peter, then asked, "Quo Vadis, Peter?"—"Where are you headed, Peter?" The tradition of the early church says Peter discontinued his flight, re-entered the city, was arrested and martyred with the faithful.

Dr. Cronin, moved by his discovery and the question enshrined there, moved to one of the chapel's short wooden pews. In this humble and obscure place he began to prayerfully consider the question, "Quo Vadis, Archibald Joseph Cronin?" He turned the question over and over in his mind.

> Was not this a question which I, or any man, might ask himself today? The thought of those past weeks of pleasure stung me. There came upon me an extraordinary sense of emptiness and dissatisfaction, an awareness, sharp as sudden pain, of how fatally I—and others like me—had become absorbed in worldly affairs. We had forgotten, or ignored, the kingdom of the spirit. In the somber nave, barely illuminated by a shaft of light stealing through the transept, I saw this, suddenly, as the blight

which lay upon mankind. Throughout the modern world men had become oblivious to the purpose of their being; they sought only for temporal honor and material grandeur. The dominant cry today was no longer "How much can I do?" but only "How much can I get?"[58]

It is still a question worth pondering. Quo Vadis? Where are you going? By what standards do you live your life? By what priorities do you make your decisions? What is your overriding goal? What do you live to achieve? For what cause would you being willing to die? Quo Vadis?

Those questions are all about wisdom. Who is foolish and who is wise? Certainly a person can be smart and not be wise, educated but still lack wisdom. The Bible says, "Where is the wise man? Where is the scholar? Where is the philosopher of this age? Has not God made foolish the wisdom of the world?" (1 Corinthians 1:20) Paul acknowledges the absence in the church of those the world considers wise and highly placed. While there are exceptions to every rule, those wise in the ways of the world often reject the message of salvation as too simplistic to be true.

The word "wisdom" is an interesting one. The Greek word is "sophes." From it we derive several common English words, including sophisticated and sophomore.

The word "sophomore" is actually a combination of two Greek words that literally mean "wise-fool." Anyone who has raised a sixteen-year-old understands the term perfectly well. No further explanation is needed.

A sophisticated person is one who is "wise in the ways of the world." Sophistication is not so easy to explain. Supposedly, sophisticated people know which fork to use and exactly what to say and what to do in formal social situations. Not so long ago (while leading a conference in Houston, Texas), Carol, I, and a couple from Wisconsin were invited by Texas friends to enjoy a wonderful dinner at the Petroleum Club located in one of Houston's downtown high-rise buildings. The company was excellent, the conversation lively, the view spectacular, and the dinner superb.

As expected, the waiter asked each person at our table for his or her preference of wine, white or red. Although unaccustomed to such surroundings, I was sophisticated enough to know that typically those eating beef order red wine, and those dining on seafood order white. I had ordered a steak fillet but without a moment's hesitation requested white wine with my meal. We had a good laugh in the car on the way back to our hotel as my friends chided me for my inappropriate selection. I responded that my palate was simply not sophisticated enough to enjoy dry red wine, so I ordered what I liked. The difference between managers and leaders, I've been told, is that managers do things right, but leaders do right things. As a Christian and as a leader I find it especially easy to ignore conventional practice in favor of what seems (as the old liturgical prayer says) "good, right, and salutary." The sophisticated choice was easy; the wise choice was more complex. What is wise is a matter of opinion.

The etymology of the Greek word for wisdom is enlightening. Some believe its origins are closely tied to the similar word "saphes," which means "clear." You may recognize that term as the root for the English word "sapphire." The clarity of a sapphire is its most important feature. The implication is that a wise person sees "clearly" in situations where others may be confused and unsure.

Who is wise and who is not? The Old Testament states several times, "The fear of the LORD is the beginning of wisdom, and knowledge of the Holy One is understanding" (Proverbs 9:10). (Cf. Psalm 111:10, Proverbs 1:7.) Not everyone accepts that definition. Some call the Lord's way a stumbling block and others call it foolishness.[59] If by being foolish it means God's ways are not the same as man's ways then the Lord would agree. He would even add, "The foolishness of God is wiser than man's wisdom, and the weakness of God is stronger than man's strength" (1 Corinthians 1:25).

Dr. Cronin had enjoyed the best the world had to offer but remained unsatisfied. When confronted by the question, "Quo Vadis?" he began to wonder who was wise and who was foolish. Suddenly the best the world had to offer seemed empty and cheap. The Scripture says life is full and satisfying when one is "wise for salvation through faith in Christ Jesus. ... thoroughly equipped for every good work" (2 Timothy 3:15, 17). In the same letter to Timothy, the apostle told his young understudy God wants all people to be saved *and come to the knowledge of truth.* God doesn't want wisdom to remain rare. He intends for it to be widespread.

Who among us hasn't experienced the same discovery of Dr. Cronin, albeit to a lesser degree? After a long day's work (or a long week's work) we may come home intent on just one thing—downtime with no distractions, no phones, no intrusions. Alone. Well, almost alone—except for that quart of ice cream or that bag of potato chips. We've earned the right. We can exercise our freedom to soothe our innermost craving. Like the man says, "You only go around once in life. Why not grab a little gusto?" And so for the next two hours we kick back and indulge.

But instead of experiencing great internal satisfaction and fulfillment after we have finished indulging, finished satisfying our innermost craving, we, like Dr. Cronin, are stung by the sharp pangs of guilt. Instinctively we know life is meant for better things. As he discovered, the greater question of our day is not "How much can we get?" but "What can we do?"

The foolishness of God is wiser than man's wisdom.

God created people to be productive, to make a difference in things that matter most. Ice cream and potato chips are not the key to fulfillment. The key to fulfillment is found in the list of values by which the Lord will assess life on the day of final judgment. People who know God's love and have been rescued from eternal death by Jesus' sacrifice will show their appreciation by serving others.

> Then the King will say to those on His right, "Come, you who are blessed by My Father; take your inheritance, the kingdom prepared for you since the creation of the world. For I was hungry and you gave Me something to eat, I was thirsty and you gave Me something to drink, I was a stranger and you invited Me in, I needed clothes and you clothed Me, I was sick and you looked after Me, I was in prison and you came to visit Me." (Matthew 25:34–36)

"The fear of the LORD is the beginning of wisdom, and knowledge of the Holy One is understanding" (Proverbs 9:10). That is wisdom. That is the way to satisfaction and peace.

Quo Vadis?

CHAPTER TWENTY-FOUR

Unity
or Disunity

The power of synthesis

How good and pleasant it is when brothers live together in unity! Psalm 133:1

Today's world hardly resembles the one God created. The book of Genesis says God walked through the Garden of Eden in the cool of the evening. We can only imagine how Adam and Eve looked forward to His visits and the opportunity to share a moment or two with their Lord.

According to the Genesis account, conditions in the garden and around the world changed dramatically after the flood. The earliest Scriptures mention nothing of rain, instead we are told a mist came up from the ground and watered the earth.[60] The Bible says our planet was enveloped by a great band of water which encircled the globe.[61] The description of the flood includes reference to those waters. Genesis chapter seven says, "On that day all the springs of the great deep burst forth, and the floodgates of the heavens were opened" (v. 11). Before the flood such a thick atmosphere may have created a greenhouse effect from one end of the earth to the other. These descriptions help explain the dinosaur age and the abundance of tropical plant life in such unlikely places as Alaska and the Middle East. Those inhospitable climates are now the world's chief storehouse of fossil fuel in the form of oil, a silent testimony to their ancient and tropical past.

The Lord's directives to Noah and his family after the flood give hints of other major changes too. Evidence suggests that before the flood people subsisted on vegetarian diets. After the flood the Lord said to Noah, "Everything that lives and moves will be food for you. Just as I gave you the green plants, I now give you everything" (Genesis 9:3). The animal world has never been the same. As an aid in their survival the Lord said of the animals, "The fear and dread of you will fall upon all the beasts of the earth and all the birds of the air, upon every creature that moves along the ground, and upon all the fish of the sea" (Genesis 9:2). Evidently the natural fear of man was not a part of created animal instincts. Survival instincts imposed by God now made all living things wary of man.

Yes, the world we live in today is different than the world God made. As Paul says, all creation has been subjected to the effect of Adam's fall and with God's children eagerly awaits the end of sin's reign on planet Earth. He wrote, "The creation waits in eager expectation for the sons of God to be revealed. For the creation was subjected to frustration, not by its own choice, but by the will of the One who subjected it, in hope that the creation itself will be liberated from its bondage to decay and brought into the glorious freedom of the children of God" (Romans 8:19–21). If sin brought such dramatic change in man's relationship to animals, the change that occurred in human relationships is even greater.

The created power of human unity was incredible, even miraculous. It was all a part of God's intended design. Soon after Adam's creation the Lord observed, "It is not good for the man to be alone" (Genesis 2:18). (I believe God always knew man had this need and the creation of woman was no afterthought. The Lord simply wanted Adam to experience loneliness in order to create a greater appreciation for its solution.)

No doubt about it, human beings were made to live in community. God made us that way. Even today, the sum total of unified talent holds greater potential than the collective talents of greater individuals. This explains why underdogs often rise up and beat superior teams.

December 7, 1941, will long be remembered in the annals of both American and Japanese history. On that day an estimated 150 to 200 planes, launched from three or four Japanese carriers, made a surprise attack on Pearl Harbor, the base of operations for the American Pacific fleet. More than 3,000 Americans lost their lives, nineteen ships were sunk or severely damaged, and nearly 200 planes were destroyed. The Japanese planes returned triumphantly to their fleet, their pilots understandably overjoyed with their success. When congratulated on his great victory, Admiral Yamamoto is said to have turned away in somber reflection. Looking off toward the horizon he responded, "You don't understand. Today we have awakened a sleeping giant." Yamamoto knew the power of unity, intent on one purpose, and motivated by a great cause.

Tragically, whenever sin enters the picture, good things can be used for evil purposes. The power of unity became a detriment rather than an asset to man. Perhaps that abuse is best seen in the construction of the Tower of Babel. The account begins with the words, "Now the whole world had one language and a common speech" (Genesis 11:1). They were united as God intended. Trouble began when they used the created power of unity for evil. As the story unfolds the descendants of Noah became more and more self-reliant. They would not heed the command of God to be "fruitful and increase in number and fill the earth" (Genesis 9:1). Instead, they wanted to build a symbol of their own fame and a monument to their own power. They refused to disperse as God had commanded. In effect, they were rejecting God, intending to control their own destiny. The story doesn't end there.

> But the LORD came down to see the city and the tower that the men were building. The LORD said, "If as one people speaking the same language they have begun to do this, then nothing they plan to do will be impossible for them. Come, let Us go down and confuse their language so they will not understand each other." So the LORD scattered them from there over all the earth, and they stopped building the city. (Genesis 11:5–8)

God commented, "If as one people speaking the same language they have begun to do this, then nothing they plan to do will be impossible for them." Even God acknowledges that the power of unity is incredible. God is not against unity, nor is He against great accomplishment. He simply cares too much to allow the created power of unity to destroy the people He loves. For that reason God created differences that make the exercise of unity nearly impossible.

For similar reasons God removed the Tree of Life from the Garden of Eden. Although His original intention was that people would live forever, when sin came into the world He graciously limited life in order to limit human pain and suffering. That tree is now located in heaven where its intended purpose is being fulfilled in a new and sinless environment. (Cf. Revelation 22:1–2.)

But just as the original gift of eternal life is now restored to those who believe in Jesus, so the created power of unity is reinstated under the authority of Christ.

- Jesus prayed for such unity. (John 17:23)
- Paul spoke of it as a blessing. (Romans 15:4)
- It comes through Christian maturity. (Ephesians 4:13)
- Forgiveness is the key. (Colossians 3:13)

Unity is an essential element of every great Christian endeavor. My wife, Carol, sings in our church choir. We have a great choir under the direction of a truly gifted and godly director. Bobby, our director, understands the created and powerful nature of unity. His greatest challenge is not raising the talents of the less musically gifted. His greatest challenge is handling the egos and abilities of those blessed with great instrumental and vocal talent. He knows from experience that what comes easily for the gifted often requires repetition and patient instruction for the others. When the choir is united it is awesome. Although I have never been to heaven, I have been in the midst of Bobby's choir when they are hitting their stride in perfect harmony. Heaven must be like that.

When the choir is preparing for a major musical presentation Bobby will distribute to the members cassette tapes which feature their vocal parts. Carol sings alto so she always has the alto cassette playing in her car. Alto is hard to sing, not because of the range, but because of the dynamic (or lack of it). Altos are to music what flour is to gravy. They contribute little to the flavor but provide the needed body. I once heard Bobby tell Carol that he just loves to hear the altos sing, and I'm sure he does. I have also heard him say the same thing to the bass section. Bobby knows "the sum total of unified talent holds greater potential than the collective talents of greater individuals."

If it were up to me, we would all sing soprano or tenor and I'd complain that the parts were too high. Bobby is wiser than that. He knows there is greater power in the unified mixture of parts than in any one chief part.

Christians must daily renew their commitment to the power of unity—unity that is established on obedience to Christ and maintained through mutual forgiveness. Incredible things— even miraculous things—occur when unity is allowed its day.

Jackie Robinson was the first black baseball player to break the color barrier in the major leagues. It took more than skill to succeed. Someone once said, "It takes skill to rise to the top, but it takes character to stay there." It also takes the help of others.

Jackie's attempt to integrate the major leagues was not warmly received by many of the other major leaguers or by the fans, even his hometown fans in Brooklyn. The year before he played in the majors, Jackie's minor league team played in the "Little World Series" against Louisville. The fans there vilified Jackie. Now that he was in the majors, all eyes were on the rookie, waiting for him to make his first mistake. The story changes, depending on the witness, but the point remains: The opposing dugouts were shouting jeers and boos at Jackie Robinson. Those moments on the field must have felt like hours. Then something unexpected happened. The Dodgers' much-loved shortstop, Pee Wee Reese (a native of Louisville), walked over to Robinson at second base. Reese put his arm around the rookie and whispered something to him. The action spoke volumes, especially coming from a southerner. In his own way, Reese was telling the abusers he was on Jackie's team, not theirs. Robinson later said that arm around his shoulder saved his career.

There is power in unity.

CHAPTER TWENTY-FIVE

First or Last

It isn't how you drive, it's how you arrive.

A
But many who are first will be last, and many who are last will be first. Matthew 19:30

mericans love to be number one. Comedians make jokes about the vice president of the United States having nothing to do. Sports fans remember who won last year's Super Bowl or World Series but don't remember whom the winner beat in the final game. Collecting cards of the best players has become more than just a hobby. Americans love winners.

In February 1950, the Associated Press ran a contest to see who sportswriters would vote as the greatest athlete of the first fifty years of the twentieth century. It was quite a contest, involving athletes from every field. Who would it be? Joe Louis or maybe Jack Dempsey—legendary boxers; Lou Gehrig—batting champion; Babe Ruth—homerun king; Jackie Robinson—the hall-of-famer who broke the color barrier in professional baseball; Bobby Jones—golf immortal; Ty Cobb—the toughest man ever to play hardball; or Red Grange—the Illinois Galloping Ghost?

The truth is none of these legendary greats was chosen. Two out of every three votes went to a Native American born in a one-room log cabin along the North Canadian River in Oklahoma. He played college sports for the now defunct Carlisle Indian School under the great coach Papa Glenn Warner. That little Indian school demolished their opponents in football and track, winning national bragging rights against the greatest teams of their day, including Harvard, Yale, and Army. The All-American Ike Eisenhower and his Army team could not stop the Indians from inflicting a humiliating 27 to 6 defeat (in a day when touchdowns counted only five points). The score might have been worse but one of the star's kickoff returns was disallowed because of an offside penalty. On the very next kick he again returned the ball the complete length of the field, this time without being recalled! The halfback called it the longest touchdown ever scored since he had to run the length of the field twice before they allowed the points. Throughout the game (and his college career for that matter) the All-American shouted out the upcoming play to the defensive team, both taunting and daring them to stop it before he ran unrestrained through their line.

His mother called him Wa-Tho-Huck, which means Bright Path. She named him right. His competitors called him the greatest athlete the world has ever known. In the Olympic Games of 1912, he won both the pentathlon and decathlon, taking first place in eight events! His great-grandfather was the renowned Indian chief Black Hawk, but he is probably better known by the last name of his Irish grandfather, Thorpe. James Francis Thorpe overcame incredible odds to be recognized as the Associated Press' greatest athlete of the first half of the century. Two out of every three votes cast named Jim the greatest of them all. Babe Ruth was the closest anyone came to second place, and he trailed in the overall voting by more than 300 points.

Life had not been easy for James. At age eight his best friend and twin bother, Charles, died of complications brought on by pneumonia. His mother died when he was twelve, and his father died two years later. He idolized his father who taught him to hunt, fish, and trap according to the old Indian customs. After his father's death, Jim felt like a man without a home.

Unsure what to do, he left Carlisle and spent a couple years drifting with some buddies who signed on with minor league baseball teams in North Carolina and Fayetteville, Arkansas. The fifteen dollars a week wasn't much money, but it paid for his meals, and he enjoyed the travel. Recruited back to college by his beloved Coach Warner, Thorpe qualified for the Olympics and won All-American honors in football the next two years. Little did he know his gridiron fame and Olympic glory would be tarnished by accusations of fraud.

Under strict A.A.U. regulations, athletes were not permitted to participate in any sport for money without forfeiting their amateur status. When his bush league career was discovered, Thorpe was stripped of all his Olympic medals, including the bronze bust and jewel-studded Viking ship he had received for his victories in the pentathlon and decathlon respectively. Neither the Norwegian nor the Swedish athlete who finished second to Thorpe in those events would accept them, believing that Thorpe was the greatest athlete in the world. Thorpe went from top of the heap to the bottom in the blink of an eye. From first to last by verdict of the judge.

Jim Thorpe had some good years left and made his living as a professional baseball player and then football player until age forty. But there came a time when things were not so secure. As age slowed his step Thorpe was forced by necessity to look for work. He hired on as a day laborer for four dollars an hour, worked as a factory watchman, and supervised activities at Chicago public parks. Just a few years before his death in 1953, Hollywood rescued him with a $25,000 contract for the story of his life. Thorpe knew what it was to be on top and end up at the bottom.[62] No wonder the apostle Paul advised the young man Timothy, "Command those who are rich in this present world not to be arrogant nor to put their hope in wealth, which is so uncertain, but to put their hope in God" (1 Timothy 6:17).

There are still those who put their hope in uncertain riches. Even if they manage to hold on to those riches until they die they may spend eternity regretting it. Time and time again Jesus reminded people that in His kingdom the first are last and the last shall be first. The point is powerfully made in the story he told about a man named Lazarus.

> There was a rich man who was dressed in purple and fine linen and lived in luxury every day. At his gate was laid a beggar named Lazarus, covered with sores and longing to eat what fell from the rich man's table. Even the dogs came and licked his sores. The time came when the beggar died and the angels carried him to Abraham's side. The rich man also died and was buried. In hell, where he was in torment, he looked up and saw Abraham far away, with Lazarus by his side. So he called to him, "Father Abraham, have pity on me and send Lazarus to dip the tip of his finger in water and cool my tongue, because I am in agony in this fire." But Abraham replied, "Son, remember that in your lifetime you received your good things, while Lazarus received bad things, but now he is comforted here and you are in agony. And besides all this, between us and you a great chasm has been fixed, so that those who want to go from here to you cannot, nor can anyone cross over from there to us". (Luke 16:19–26)

God turns everything around. Riches mean nothing to Him. In fact He warns people over and over about the deadly trap of success and riches which may rob them of the most important things. The prophet asked, "Why spend money on what is not bread, and your labor on what does not satisfy?"

(Isaiah 55:2) And Jesus said it was easier for a camel to go through the eye of a needle than for a rich man to gain entrance to heaven. In the here and now, people fear not having enough and are rarely satisfied. Jesus said that attitude is all wrong. The danger is in having too much, not in having too little. Anything that weakens a person's reliance on the Lord has the power to threaten his salvation.

Lazarus, in his need, leaned on the Lord for his comfort and strength. The self-sufficient rich man had no need for God. The rich man was rich in things. Lazarus was rich in things that mattered. Things are not of themselves evil or good. There is no special merit in poverty and nothing especially sinister about wealth. But the Bible suggests that unhealthy attitudes about money are all too common. Paul did *not* say, "Money is the root of all evil." It was *the love of* money that threatens faith. "Some people," he said, "eager for money, have wandered from the faith and pierced themselves with many griefs." He urges better goals for Timothy. "But you, man of God, flee from all this, and pursue righteousness, godliness, faith, love, endurance and gentleness. Fight the good fight of the faith" (1 Timothy 6:10–12).

Two of the most haunting questions Jesus ever asked were, "What good will it be for a man if he gains the whole world, yet forfeits his soul? Or what would a man give in exchange for his soul?" (Matthew 16:26) Given a day to think about it, too many would be glad to furnish a list: a fine home, several nice cars, a handsome spouse, friends, reputation, power, privilege, and good health.

But God works in unexpected ways. Jesus said if we seek the kingdom of God first He will provide for all our needs. People tend to think, "It's up to me to provide for all my needs. Then I will have time for God." When you start with God, living and working according to His will as revealed in His Word, you have His assurance that your needs will be met. Those who strive after perceived needs may forfeit their greatest need. When you live according to God's plan you're assured you'll have it all, especially God's most important blessings. When you live according to different priorities you run the risk of failure in both areas.

When Jesus taught that the first would be last and the last would be first He was not talking only about wealth. He was also talking about status. Sometimes, the religious people are the hardest ones to save. Jesus said, "I tell you the truth, the tax collectors and the prostitutes are entering the kingdom of God ahead of you. For John came to you to show you the way of righteousness, and you did not believe him, but the tax collectors and the prostitutes did. And even after you saw this, you did not repent and believe him" (Matthew 21:31–32).

Those who have nothing are more appreciative for the things they receive. When it comes to salvation, those who know they are lost have the greatest appreciation for their salvation. Conversely, those who live a good life sometimes take comfort in their behavior and lose a deep appreciation for the importance of Jesus' death on their behalf.

I grew up as a member of a country church in the farm belt of Indiana. To say I was raised in a conservative environment would be an understatement. No one locked their cars or their homes, and if your dog got lost, people across town would call to tell you they had seen him running with some strays. My family worshiped in the same building my great-grandparents had helped build more than 100 years earlier. Church was always well-attended. Even as a young boy, I could tell a visitor from a regular member. The visitors opened their hymnals. The hymnal we used had been published in 1941. The regular members knew all the orders of service—and most of the hymns—by heart. Except for some hymns, my folks could actively participate through an entire worship service without ever opening their books.

Occasionally, for variation, the pastor would use a portion of the Confessional Service to prepare the congregation for receiving the Lord's Supper. On those occasions, we all had to take out our hymnals and follow along. The Confessional Service was too long and infrequently used to be memorized by even the most devoted members. In place of the usual prayers of repentance, the Confessional Service asked five specific questions about attitudes, intentions, and beliefs. I liked its direct approach and was always glad to participate when the pastor used it. It began with the pastor reading from a section of the service called "The Exhortation."

The pastor would say, "Dearly beloved: Forasmuch as we purpose to come to the Holy Supper of our Lord Jesus Christ, it becometh us diligently to examine ourselves ..." The next paragraph seemed to negate the first. It continues, "But if we thus examine ourselves, we shall find nothing in us but sin and death, from which we can in no wise set ourselves free." The answer to this quandary followed, "Therefore our Lord Jesus Christ hath had mercy upon us and hath taken upon Himself our nature, that so He might fulfill for us the whole will and Law of God and for us and for our deliverance suffer death and all that we by our sins have deserved."[63]

"But if we thus examine ourselves, we shall find nothing in us but sin and death ..." Luther had some interesting things to say about people who practiced personal examination and afterwards felt pretty good about their spiritual condition. To those who felt confession was needed by unbelievers but was wasted on Christians who knew and did God's will, Luther wrote:

No better advice can be given than this: first, he should pinch his body to see if he still has flesh and blood. Then he should believe what the Scriptures say of it in Galatians 5 and Romans 7. Second, he should look around to see whether he is still in the world, and remember that there will be no lack of sin and trouble, as the Scriptures say in John 15–16 and in 1 John 2 and 5. Third, he will certainly have the devil also around him, who with his lying and murdering day and night will let him have no peace, within or without, as the Scriptures picture him in John 8 and 16; 1 Peter 5; Ephesians 6; and 2 Timothy 2.[64]

It's like children lining up for lunch at school. The strongest and quickest trip over themselves and others making sure they are first in line. They believe in the survival of the fittest and advancement through self-promotion. What would happen if after all the pushing and shoving was over, the teacher would say, "Today we will let the back of the line lead us to the cafeteria?" Those in heaven will not be there because they pushed themselves to the front of the line. Those who are greatest in the kingdom of God are those who have the greatest appreciation for His grace.

The Lord's ways are not the ways of the world. In His world the first will be last and the last will be first. No wonder Paul said:

"Whatever was to my profit I now consider loss for the sake of Christ. What is more, I consider everything a loss compared to the surpassing greatness of knowing Christ Jesus my Lord, for whose sake I have lost all things. I consider them rubbish, that I may gain Christ and be found in Him, not having a righteousness of my own that comes from the law, but that which is through faith in Christ". (Philippians 3:7–9)

Epilogue

Have you noticed that some people get all the breaks while others struggle just to get by? The fortunate few know what to say and what to do while the rest of us flounder and struggle along. Why?

- What's the key to maintaining a strong and healthy marriage?
- What single factor creates the greatest demand for products and service?
- How do smart executives keep employees motivated and loyal?
- What distinguishes a great teacher from a good teacher?
- What skill is considered essential for success at the top?
- Why do the brightest people often end up working for their intellectual inferiors?
- What can make a mediocre speech great?
- And, dare I risk it? What makes some books easy to read and others an exercise in endurance?

The answer is **communication**. The Latin root word for communication means "to share" or "to have in common." The same Latin word is the root for our English word "commune." In order for people to come together, for them to share common attitudes, values, and faith, communication is required. The better the communication, the better the communion.

No group is motivated to share their faith, values, and attitudes more effectively than Christians—especially Christians who love nonbelievers. Why is it so frustrating? Why can't we connect? What keeps us from succeeding?

Is it just a communication breakdown, pure and simple? It happens. Even experts can fail when it comes to the difficult task of communicating their meaning. What seems so clear to the communicator may say something entirely different to the audience. Consider the following examples of miscommunication by people who get paid to communicate.

From the Stow, Ohio, Hudson Hub Times:

Have Fun At Prom; Don't Drink, Do Drugs

From the Houston Chronicle:

States Target Women, Children in Effort to Promote Deer Hunting

From New Orleans based public relations firm, P.R. PR, Inc.:

Autos Killing 110 a Day, Let's Resolve to Do Better
Miners Refuse to Work after Death
Prostitutes Appeal to Pope

From the Rochester, NY Democrat & Chronicle:

Fish Lurk in Streams

From the Arizona Daily Star:

Deer Interfering with Jets Being Shot at Philly Airport

From the Chicago Tribune:

Chemotherapy Fears Increase after Death

From Editor's Workshop, by Peter Jacobi
(in a column about clarity):

Del Monte Foods to Can 150 Employees
Iraqi Head Seeks Arms

News report from the Internet (source of origin unknown):
Enraged Cow Injures Farmer with Ax
From the Daily Local News (Chester County, PA):

> Perhaps the cruelest tragedy in the death yesterday of James E. Dever is that had it happened a few minutes later, he might still be alive.[65]

Miscommunication happens, even at the hand of professional communicators. But miscommunication doesn't adequately explain the difficulty of sharing Christian beliefs with nonbelievers.

Sharing the Christian faith is unlike any other form of communication. It requires mediation, not excellence of speech. The apostle Paul talked about this unique aspect of Christian witnessing in his letter to the church at Corinth. In the first chapter of his letter, Paul openly admits that proclaiming the crucified Jesus to be the Jewish Messiah and Savior of the world was frequently ineffective. A crucified Messiah was a "stumbling block" to the Jews and "foolishness" to nonJews. Paul noticed those who accepted Jesus were typically not the brightest, the wealthiest, nor the most successful people in society. He explained, "God chose the foolish things of the world to shame the wise; God chose the weak things of the world to shame the strong. He chose the lowly things of this world and the despised things—and the things that are not—to nullify the things that are, so that no one may boast before Him" (1 Corinthians 1:27–29).

Paul freely admits that not everyone has an easy time accepting the faith that Christians have often died to defend. Things like riches, position, and worldly intelligence can be stumbling blocks to those who are self-reliant and self-satisfied.

There is another important truth that impacts the ability to communicate the faith effectively in a nonbelieving world. Paul called it the Holy Spirit factor. It might help to know that Paul, an expert in the Old Testament law and a hard-working, passionate zealot, was not the most confident or dynamic communicator. Once, when he was speaking, a young man in his audience sank into a deep sleep, lost his balance, and fell from a third-story window! Fortunately for both speaker and listener, Paul's prayers on his behalf were granted and the boy fully recovered.

It should comfort us to know that Paul readily admitted his inability to effectively communicate, even when talking about Jesus. He told the Corinthian Christians, "I came to you in weakness and fear, and with much trembling. My message and my preaching were not with wise and persuasive words, but with a demonstration of the Spirit's power, so that your faith might not rest on men's wisdom, but on God's power" (1 Corinthians 2:3–5).

What comfort! What a relief! The conversion of the lost does not rest on our ability to plead the case for Christ. When Christians lovingly speak God's truth, the Holy Spirit accompanies their words and goes to work on the hearts of the lost. No Christian will ever argue anyone into heaven. The Lord only asks Christians to live their lives sincerely and to be ready to give witness to the hope that they have in Jesus Christ—nothing more, nothing less. Changing hearts is God's business, not ours.

Now, when I see a nonbeliever get agitated over a Christian's simple witness to the Bible's truth, I just smile. A nonbeliever's degree of agitation can be an indication of the Lord at work. God's Word has the power to prick the conscience and cut the heart of those who resist. By the way some people respond, I believe that having your conscience pricked and your heart cut must be a painful thing.

The Old Testament prophet said, "No man can redeem the life of another or give to God a ransom for him—the ransom for a life is costly, no payment is ever enough" (Psalm 49:7–8). Jesus said, "He who listens to you listens to Me; he who rejects you rejects Me; but he who rejects Me rejects Him who sent Me" (Luke 10:16). Salvation is work Christians can't do without the power of the Holy Spirit working through the Word of God. As Christians we can take no credit for those who are saved. Likewise, we should take no blame for those who reject the message of the truth.

A young man of our congregation was recently commended for his helpfulness in leading and teaching other teenage boys about Jesus. As a compliment, one of the members said he would one day make a fine Christian leader. Without much thought, the young man replied, "I am not a leader. I am just a follower of Christ. If others want to follow along with me, they are more than welcome." What a great answer. Refusing to accept the burden and responsibility for tending the souls of others, he placed the responsibility where it belonged, at the feet of Jesus. A Christian's job is to be faithful, not successful.

The issues of faith are not going to suddenly disappear. No great teacher is ever going to defend the faith in such an effective way that the whole world will believe. Not even the discovery of Noah's ark in the mountains of Turkey would bring about worldwide conversions. How many people saw the miracles of Jesus? How many sons of Israel were shown how completely the Savior's life fulfilled all the Old Testament messianic prophesies? Though convinced, they remained unconvinced. The foolishness of Christian beliefs will always seem foolish in the world of the nonbeliever.

Christians should not feel greatly burdened to make their beliefs more palatable to those whose eyes see but do not perceive and whose ears hear but do not comprehend (cf. Matthew 13:15–16). It is enough to believe and to tell the simple truth in simple words. The strength of God's Word is deceptive and subtle. Like flimsy paper, easily crumpled and discarded, its edge can still slice the most callused hands. God's Word has an edge to it.

When Peter spoke the truth about Jesus to the skeptics and Jewish legalists in Jerusalem they were "*cut to the heart* and said to Peter and the other apostles, 'Brothers what shall we do?' " (Acts 2:37, emphasis added) Luke tells us, "Those who accepted his message were baptized, and about three thousand were added to their number that day" (v. 41). God has not changed nor has His Word lost any of its power. The apostle said, "The word of God is living and active. Sharper than any double-edged sword, it penetrates even to dividing soul and spirit, joints and marrow; it judges the thoughts and attitudes of the heart" (Hebrews 4:12). God's truth, like a sword in its sheath, looks harmless and archaic. But unsheathed and loosed, the truth always merits respect. Christian right may look wrong in the rational world of a nonbeliever. Share your beliefs anyway. The truth spoken in love has an edge that can cut the hardest heart.

Endnotes

[1] George Diaz, "Playing by God's Rules," *The Orlando Sentinel,* December 29, 1996. Used by permission.

[2] Robert Frost, "Mending Wall." Public Domain.

[3] The story of President Lincoln and Edwin Stanton is adapted from Donald Phillips, *Lincoln on Leadership,* (New York, New York: Warner Books, 1992), page 30 and Paul Lee Tan, *Encyclopedia of 7,700 Illustrations: Signs of the Times,* (Chicago, Illinois: Donnelley and Sons, Inc., 1979) 133. Used by permission.

[4] Lance Davidson, *The Ultimate Reference Book: The Wits Thesaurus,* (New York, New York: Avon Books, 1994) 94. Max Reger (1873–1916) wrote the letter to the critic Rudolph Louis in response to his review in *Munchener Neuste Nahrichten,* February 7, 1906. Used by permission.

[5] Brian Duffy, "The Mad Bomber?" *U.S. News & World Report,* Copyright © April 15, 1996, U.S. News & World Report, page 28ff. Used by permission.

[6] Rob Howe, "For the Greater Good," *People Weekly,* vol. 45, no. 16, April 22, 1996, 50. Used by permission.

[7] Evan Thomas, "Blood Brothers," *Newsweek,* vol. 127, no. 17, April 22, 1996, 28. Used by permission.

[8] Adapted from *Great Disasters: Dramatic True Stories of Nature's Awesome Powers*, (Pleasantville, New York: The Readers Digest Association, 1989) 146–49.

[9] Jim Ness, "Quicksand!" *Guideposts,* May 1996, 25ff. Used by permission.

[10] Hatred is the opposite of love, described here using terms contrasting those Paul used to define love in 1 Corinthians 13.

[11]From THE TRUE JOY OF POSITIVE LIVING by Norman Vincent Peale, page 160. Copyright © 1984 by Norman Vincent Peale. Used by permission of William Morrow & Company, Inc.

[12]Ibid., 231.

[13]Marshall Broomhall, editor, *Hudson Taylor's Legacy,* (London, England: Hodder and Stoughton, 1974), 8. (Copyright by The Overseas Advisory Fellowship, first printed in 1931 by The China Inland Mission, now OMF International.) Used by permission.

[14]Ibid., 60.

[15]Nancy Leigh DeMoss, *The Rebirth of America,* (Philadelphia, Pennsylvania: The DeMoss Foundation, 1986) 191. Used by permission.

[16]**HAPPY TRAILS** by Dale Evans, Copyright © 1951 & 1952 by Paramount-Roy Rogers Music Co., Inc. Copyright renewed 1979 & 1980 and assigned to Paramount-Roy Rogers Music Co., Inc. Used by permission.

[17]Elise Miller Davis, *The Answer Is God: The Inspiring Personal Story of Dale Evans & Roy Rogers,* (Old Tappan, New Jersey: Pyramid Publications, a Fleming Revell Company by arrangement with McGraw-Hill Books, 1955), 7.

[18]Ibid., 252.

[19]Ibid., 268.

[20]Dr. Frank Harrington, pastor of Peachtree Presbyterian Church in Atlanta, Georgia. Used by permission.

[21]Ashley Hale, "The Stewardship Lesson of Lessons: Givers Are Winners," *The Clergy Journal,* September 1982, 43. Used by permission.

[22]John Lukacs, "The Dangerous Summer of 1940," *World War II— The Best of American Heritage,* edited by Stephen W. Sears, (New York, New York: Houghton Mifflin Co., 1991), 3. Used by permission.

[23]Henry Wadsworth Longfellow, "I Heard the Bells on Christmas Day." Public Domain.

[24]From THE DIARY OF A YOUNG GIRL THE DEFINITIVE EDITION

by Anne Frank. Otto H. Frank & Mirjam Pressler, Editors, translated by Susan Massotty. English translation copyright © 1995 by Doubleday, a division of Bantam Doubleday Dell Publishing Group, Inc. Used by permission of Doubleday, a division of Bantam Doubleday Dell Publishing Group, Inc. Page 6. (Saturday, June 20, 1942)

[25]Ibid., 8. (Saturday, June 20, 1942)

[26]Ibid., 18. (Sunday morning, July 5, 1942)

[27]Ibid., 332. (Saturday, July 15, 1944)

[28]Henry Wadsworth Longfellow, "I Heard the Bells on Christmas Day." Public Domain.

[29]In the late 1960s and early 1970s I had been taught what is called a "higher-critical form of Bible study" which held that Moses did not write the first five books of the Bible. We were taught those earliest books of the Bible were actually written at the end of the Old Testament period by scribes using various oral and written sources called JEDP, which stood for the Jahwist, Elohist, Deuteronomist, and Priestly sources. By God's grace I no longer accept higher-critical theories nor are they being taught anymore in my denomination's colleges and seminaries.

[30]Rev. Joe Wright, Central Christian Church, Wichita, Kansas. Used by permission.

[31]Martin Luther, *Luther's Small Catechism with Explanation,* Copyright © 1986, 1991 by Concordia Publishing House, St. Louis, Missouri, page 12. All rights reserved.

[32]Compare Hosea 11:1 to Matthew 2:15.

[33]Compare Isaiah 9:1–2 to Matthew 4:15.

[34]Compare Micah 5:2 to Matthew 2:5–6.

[35]Compare Genesis 35:19, 48:7 and Jeremiah 31:15 to Matthew 2:18.

[36]See John 1:45–49.

[37]Rev. David Mulder, "Actual Quotes from U.S. Army Officer Evaluation Reports," *CrossTalk,* Concordia Publishing House, St. Louis, MO, June/July 1996. All rights reserved.

[38]Romans 12:1

[39]Elisabeth Elliot, *Through Gates of Splendor,* Copyright © 1956, 1957, 1981 by Elisabeth Elliot, title page. Used by permission.

[40]Ibid., 104.

[41]Ibid., 165.

[42]Martha Snell Nicholson, *Her Lamp of Faith: Selected Poems of Martha Snell Nicholson*, compiled by F.J. Wiens. (Chicago, Illinois: Moody Press, 1968). Used by permission.

[43]Elisabeth Elliot, *Through Gates of Splendor,* page 241. Used by permission.

[44]Ibid., viii.

[45]General Chuck Yeager and Leo Janos, *Yeager, An Autobiography,* (New York, New York: Bantam Books, Copyright © 1985 by Yeager, Inc.), 318–319. Used by permission.

[46]Ibid., 319.

[47]David Burns, "Aim for Success, Not Perfection," *Psychology Today,* November 1980. Reprinted with permission from *Psychology Today Magazine,* Copyright © 1980 (Sussex Publishers, Inc.).

[48] "Strive for Perfection—OR ELSE!" *The Working Communicator,* August 1996, (Chicago, Illinois: Lawrence Ragan Communications, Inc.). Reprinted with permission of *The Working Communicator,* Lawrence Ragan Communications, Inc., 212 W. Superior, Chicago, IL 60610.

[49]Text: Paul Gerhardt (1667), "Come Your Hearts and Voices Raising," hymn 90:1, 2, *The Lutheran Hymnal,* Copyright © 1941 by Concordia Publishing House, St. Louis, Missouri. All rights reserved.

[50]Harold S. Kushner, *When Bad Things Happen to Good People,* (New York, New York: Schocken Books, Copyright © 1981 by Harold S. Kushner). In a chapter entitled, "God Can't Do Everything, But He Can Do Some Important Things," the author suggests prayer is not for the sake of getting well. He counsels, "He didn't make you have this problem [fate did], and He doesn't want you to go on having it, but He can't make it go away. That is something

which is too hard even for God" (page 129). The value of prayer, he concludes, is "You discover people around you, and God beside you, and strength within you to help you survive the tragedy" (page 131).

[51]Text: Symphonia Sirenum, Köln, 1695; Francis Pott, tr., alt. "The Strife Is O'er, the Battle Done," hymn 143:1, *Lutheran Worship,* © Copyright 1982 by Concordia Publishing House, St. Louis, Missouri. All rights reserved.

[52]*Missouri Laws Relating to Child Abuse and Neglect,* **Chapter 1, Laws in Force and Construction of Statutes** 210.110. Definitions.–As used in sections 210.109 to 210.165, and sections 210.180 to 210.183, the following terms mean: (1) "Abuse," any physical injury, sexual abuse, or emotional abuse inflicted on a child other than by accidental means by those responsible for the child's care, custody, and control except that discipline including spanking, administered in a reasonable manner, shall not be construed to be abuse.

[53]The Greek word implies scourging or whipping, coming from a root word meaning "to make contact." It implies that God's discipline involves active intervention when a child He loves wanders from the truth.

[54]Paul Zimmerman, *Darwin, Evolution and Creation,* (St. Louis, Missouri: Concordia Publishing House, 1959) 96–97. All rights reserved.

[55]Albert Sippert, *Evolution Is Not Scientific: 32 Reasons Why* (previously published as *From Eternity to Eternity: Evolution Is Not a Science*), (Mankato, Minnesota: Sippert Publishing Company, 1989) 270. Used by permission.

[56]Ibid.

[57]Excerpted with permission from "Quo Vadis," by A.J. Cronin, *Reader's Digest,* December 1951. Copyright ©1951 by The Readers Digest Assn., Inc. Page 41.

[58]Ibid., 42.

[59]1 Corinthians 1:20–24

[60]Genesis 2:6 as translated in the KJV and NASB. Original language favors the translation "mist."

[61]Genesis 1:6–7

[62]Adapted from Gene Schoor, *The Jim Thorpe Story,* (New York, New York: Julian Messner Publishers, Simon and Schuster, 1951).

[63]*The Lutheran Hymnal,* Copyright © 1941 by Concordia Publishing House, St. Louis, Missouri, page 47. All rights reserved.

[64]Martin Luther, *Luther's Small Catechism with Explanation,* Copyright © 1986, 1991 by Concordia Publishing House, St. Louis, Missouri, page 42. All rights reserved.

[65]"Humorous Headlines and Other Language Matters," *The Working Communicator,* July 1996, (Chicago, Illinois: Lawrence Ragan Communications, Inc.). Reprinted with permission of *The Working Communicator,* Lawrence Ragan Communications, Inc., 212 W. Superior, Chicago, IL 60610.